Therapeutic Meditations
40 Days and 40 Nights to Change

For Hilda
you'd I'm sure. P.S.
two of my favorites.
the way you both look
your faith is inspiring.
the joy you share

Dr. John D. Lentz

preaches a powerful
sermon of love

John 10/31/05

Therapeutic Meditations
40 Days and 40 Nights to Change

All rights Reserved @ 2003 by John D. Lentz

Healing Words Press

Address for information:
Healing Words Press
230 East Maple
Jeffersonville, IN
47130

ISBN: 0-9740978-0-2

Therapeutic Meditations

40 Days and 40 Nights to Change

Dr. John D. Lentz

Healing Words Press
Jeffersonville, IN

—*Table of Contents*—

Acknowledgments

I want to thank Annie Van Vooren for her belief in the Gospel and in me. A stellar volunteer at the Kentucky Correctional Institute for Women for several years, Annie, by her gentle nudging, quietly initiated this project.

Jeff Zeig, Ph.D., gave invaluable assistance through his unwavering belief in my abilities and in this project. Jeff is a therapist, author, publisher and the founder and director of the Milton H. Erickson Foundation. Jeff is also responsible for leading and teaching me how to be more therapeutic in my messages. His friendship, mentoring and assistance are a guiding principle for how I work and live. Jeff's accomplishments, ability, talent and willingness to befriend me continue to inspire and motivate me.

I owe a similar debt to David Steere, Ph.D. David's guidance, friendship, encouragement and mentoring have been and continue to be a dominant force in my life. I first met David when he was on the faculty at the Louisville Presbyterian Theological Seminary where I was a student. David's work, faith, and lifestyle continue to influence many of my personal and professional decisions. I consider his friendship over the years to be one of the great blessings of my life.

Credit also goes to Betty Kassulke (Warden of the Kentucky Correctional Institute for Women, retired) whose faith as demonstrated in practical daily living and personal integrity continues to inspire me. Her deep spiritual commitment and belief in me humbles me and helps me persevere in my projects.

This project was possible only because of the continued support and encouragement of my wife Debra, who inspires me with her quiet devotion to God and her willingness to put her faith into practice in everyday practical situations. My son Seth and daughter Stacey deserve much appreciation for their encouragement, faith and practical suggestions.

The following people have continued to be supportive about this and other projects: Sandy McCauley, Anne Mason, Monty Hall, Teresa Lloyd, Sherry Steinbock, Sue O'Malley, Mike Rankin, Abby Flint, Maria Escalante Cortina, Steven Melton and Tammy Rhea.

I very much appreciate the editing, forward and encouragement given by Diane Cameron Lawrence. She also deserves much credit for naming the meditations.

In similar fashion, the women at the Kentucky Correctional Institute for Women who typed these meditations initially (and who had to read my difficult handwriting) deserve special thanks and appreciation. Their names are written in my mind and heart even if to respect their privacy they cannot be mentioned here. Bill Wells deserves much credit for donating the photo for the front cover. Finally, I am grateful to the inmates of the Kentucky Correctional Institution for Women for their honest responses to these meditations and for their faith that taught me so much. It was their appreciation for the work I did and their willingness to change and to grow that inspired me and prompted me to continue to find ways to help people. It is easy to be thus inspired when you see others working so hard to overcome almost insurmountable life difficulties. They continue to be in my prayers.

Forward

In acting as editor for John Lentz's sermon-essays, I have had the privilege for the last year of surrounding myself with some mighty positive and esteem-building words. As I worked on this project, I found myself believing more and more in my own potential, in the potential of a close relationship to God and in the great amount of goodness it is possible to experience in life.

It was not always like this for me. And while I do not offer a full personal testimonial here, I do offer this, in the hope that in the challenges (also sometimes called hardships) of your personal journey, you may find the kinship of understanding.

Some people seem to lead charmed lives. I haven't. I've had my share of heart-ripping grief that tore me asunder, experiences such as job loss, betrayals of trust, authority abuse, infertility and watching a beloved parent suffer through a long, slow decline toward death. There was a period in my forties where I really wasn't so sure that I would make it to the other side, so many things had piled up, like cement blocks upon very tired shoulders. During this time, I searched often and, I felt, in vain for hope.

It strikes me that hope is the most earthly of the three theological virtues, the others being faith and love. The latter two seem more heavenly to me, like gifts angels bring to us. Hope is the one most easily torn apart by life experiences and, for me, at least, the one regained with the most difficulty. My intense search for hope was almost comical at one point as I asked nearly everyone I knew—friends, ministers and colleagues—my Big Question. "Where do you find hope?" And: "Did you ever lose it? Did you find it again?" I was like a puzzled child who was sure she could find the end of the rainbow if she just kept walking toward the horizon.

I have found that Dr. Lentz has much wisdom about the true challenges of life. This is not some "Pollyanna" message in this book. After working with inmates at the women's prison in Kentucky for more than 20 years, Dr. Lentz is fully aware of the real grit of life: its tremendous challenges, its deep valleys of despair, the dark places where hope seems nowhere to be found. This knowledge fuels his wisdom and makes his words more accessible to us. I for one am not much for easy platitudes. They leave me feeling like someone has put a Band-aid on an arterial bleed.

No, these words are substantive, founded in Scripture and its poetic wisdom, founded in a lifetime of counseling sad and hurt people and in discovering what works for them and what doesn't, founded in a belief that when we commit ourselves to God's truth and when we help each other, we can find our way to the Light.

I believe with all my heart and my entire mind and all my soul that there is a deep and abiding truth in life. The expression of it in life's moments is where I have begun to glimpse hope: in healers who commit to salvage operations in prisons, in volunteers who travel across the globe to work in impoverished health clinics, in activists who fight to protect our planet, in the person who stops on a highway to pick up a lost and bewildered dog, in those who offer the beleaguered refuge from the storm.

What I finally learned through my trials is that when you cannot find hope turn to love. It is there, in love—and only there, I believe—where hope can grow when it seems lost to us.

My wish for you is that you may find the help and encouragement I so sorely needed and began to find. May you find your way to faith and love and yes, to hope.

Diane Cameron Lawrence
Louisville, Kentucky
August 2002

Introduction

This is a different kind of self-help book. It contains a different type of meditation sermon than you'll find in other places. Each of these meditations was written to evoke and precipitate positive change by speaking more at an implied level than in direct ways, though many positive, direct messages are included. The reason for this type of writing is contained in the Shaker proverb that says, "What logic didn't get us into, logic won't get us out of."

In other words, this is a spiritual path. The logic of our minds cannot put together all by themselves the pieces of the change puzzle. In order to change, we need spiritual guidance and help. If you follow this path, then it is very likely that you will improve your relationship with God. Yet along the way, you will simply feel better and live and think more positively. Consciously, you may not remember the details of these meditations. That's all right; they are intended to have an effect that occurs subtly, over time, and without memory of detail. All you need to do is to read and absorb the meditations, along with the Scriptures upon which they are based.

Using our conscious, intentional mind to change has been vastly over-rated. If deciding consciously to make positive changes worked well, every New Year's Resolution would be powerful and positive. While they may start out that way, resolutions tend not to stick. When we attempt change—when we're trying to stop an addictive habit or change a destructive behavior, for example—we need more than the conscious process of decision-making. We even need more than tons of willpower. Genuine freedom from addictions, compulsions and dysfunctional thinking requires knowledge and subtle shifts in our thinking. This shift involves more attitudinal change than it does conscious decision-making and willpower.

Making changes by drawing closer to God and allowing spiritual change is a powerful method that brings about even more blessings and rewards than anyone could consciously anticipate beforehand. These meditations use spiritual resources and very sophisticated therapeutic models that are on the cutting edge of psychotherapy. I hope that you will appreciate the irony that these sophisticated methods mirror and actually employ practices used in the Bible. You may like the way it is said in Ecclesiastes: "There is nothing new under the sun." Ecclesiastes used methods similar to these meditations to alter the reader's emotions and attitudes toward healthy living.

Making change is a process. Very few conscious decisions alone are responsible for real change. Usually, when it appears on the outside that a person has simply made a decision and changed, there is really something more going on. It usually meant the culmination of many small decisions that began with a desire for a better and different life. The decision then progressed along very predictable lines toward the change. Then comes the maintenance of the change. While all this was going on underneath, an observer might not have seen much going on. A seed that is planted doesn't appear until the seed sprouts and breaks the surface of the soil. Yet much has happened for that seed to sprout—the right combination of temperature, light and rain. Decisions are much like that seed. They grow long before you will see them breaking the surface, that is, causing obvious change.

Every one of these daily meditations was prayerfully and thoughtfully compiled to be as helpful in producing change as words can be. Biblical word patterns and styles have been employed as often as possible. The whole point is to free the reader from the cultural and psychological blocks to successful living. In other words, this book is a tool for you to use that can assist you in allowing God, through your faith and through Scripture, to help you make healthy changes, changes that bring maximum joy, peace, happiness and love.

At times, these daily thoughts may seem sermon-like. That is because they started out as sermons. They were written originally to assist the incarcerated women at the Kentucky Correctional Institute for Women to heal, grow, change and let go of the thinking that brought them to the prison. Many of these women did make these changes, and others certainly improved their lives, their thinking and then finally, their experiences. The approaches used here are not only for the incarcerated, though. They are for all of us. Actually, many of the messages never were for just the inmates; outside visitors often attended our Sunday services. They realized the services were unique and appreciated the worshipful attitude of the incarcerated women. The atmosphere often was charged with a very positive, inspirational force. I like to call it faith.

The approaches and techniques presented here are the culmination of many years' efforts to find the most helpful way of using words and sermons. As I developed these sermons, I re-examined everything I had learned and read about writing sermons. I used sources from psychotherapy and linguistic analysis. Everything was evaluated by these standards: Does it help people? Is it effective? Is it in line with the Bible? The result I came up with revised completely my understanding, theory and format of sermon writing. Today, my sermons bear little resemblance to the traditional sermons I wrote early in my career.

The sermons were delivered to the main population at the prison. Then, we typed them up and delivered them to women in cellblock. (Inmates in cellblock cannot attend outside activities.) Some of the women humbled me by telling me that they read and re-read many of the sermons, sometimes every day for a week. Sometimes it was all they had to read. That alone inspired me to make the sermons the best they could be. Many women sent them home to their families and friends on a regular basis. I would get wonderful comments like, "Grandma really liked your sermon," or "Aunt Jean agreed with you about addictions." Over time, other people—prison staff, volunteers, etc.—wanted copies, too.

I began to realize that perhaps there was something in these sermons that was helping many kinds of people. Each time I discovered that a particular approach or technique helped, I refined it and used it often. Over the years, I put more effort into using words to encourage the type of healing the Bible is designed to bring to people. I evaluated the sermons for therapeutic value and effect, as well as for their true reflection of Scripture. During one two-year period, I consulted with one of the world's leading psychotherapists and authorities on the use of words for initiating change. Every part of how a message could be used to initiate change was analyzed and then cultivated. I recorded every sermon and we evaluated it for its therapeutic effectiveness. The organizing principle always was: Is it helpful?

All of this said, the real power in this process was the Lord. This entire project's development has been guided by my persistent and deeply held belief that the Bible is a book of healing for the believer. The principles that were distilled from psychotherapy and used here therapeutically all originated in Scripture. The needs of the women in prison inspired a more in-depth and intentional use of Scripture to bring relief, help and healing. It was my gift to them and now, to you.

Forty is a symbolic number in the Bible. It represents sacredness and divinely initiated change. You may remember that it rained for 40 days and 40 nights, a period that initiated a major change. You might also remember that for 40 days and nights Moses fasted and was with the Lord receiving the commandments. This time also initiated a major change. You very well might remember that Jesus fasted for 40 days and nights in the wilderness at the start of his ministry. Forty is a symbolic number that represents completion and sacredness.

It is my prayer that your journey will also be sacred and complete, and will lead to you being even more thankful to God and appreciative of His word.

Rev. John D. Lentz

Editor's note:

In most cases, Biblical citations come from the New Revised Standard Version of the Bible. Occasionally, because they were more familiar or more poetic, citations from the Revised Standard Version were used.

Both the author and the editor believe in gender-neutral thinking about God. However, it can be cumbersome in writing to constantly avoid the use of a pronoun in reference to God. For ease and familiarity, we made the decision to refer to God as "He," though no elevation of the male gender over the female is intended.

Some discretion was used in capitalization of other words and phrases.

Abbreviations

The following abbreviations are used for the books of the Bible:

Old Testament

		New Testament	
Gen	Genesis	Mt	Matthew
Ex	Exodus	Mk	Mark
Lev	Leviticus	Lk	Luke
Num	Numbers	Jn	John
Deut	Deuteronomy	Acts	Acts of the Apostles
Josh	Joshua	Rom	Romans
Judg	Judges	1 Cor	1 Corinthians
Ruth	Ruth	2 Cor	2 Corinthians
1 Sam	1 Samuel	Gal	Galatians
2 Sam	2 Samuel	Eph	Ephesians
1 Kings	1 Kings	Phil	Philippians
2 Kings	2 Kings	Col	Colossians
1 Chr	1 Chronicles	1 Thess	1 Thessalonians
2 Chr	2 Chronicles	2 Thess	2 Thessalonians
Ezra	Ezra	1 Tim	1 Timothy
Neh	Nehemiah	2 Tim	2 Timothy
Esth	Esther	Titus	Titus
Job	Job	Philem	Philemon
Ps	Psalms	Heb	Hebrews
Prov	Proverbs	Jas	James
Eccl	Ecclesiastes	1 Pet	1 Peter
Song	Song of Solomon	2 Pet	2 Peter
Isa	Isaiah	1 Jn	1 John
Jer	Jeremiah	2 Jn	2 John
Lam	Lamentations	3 Jn	3 John
Ezek	Ezekiel	Jude	Jude
Dan	Daniel	Rev	Revelations
Hos	Hosea		
Joel	Joel		
Am	Amos		
Ob	Obadiah		
Jon	Jonah		
Mic	Micah		
Nah	Nahum		
Hab	Habakkuk		
Zeph	Zephaniah		
Hag	Haggai		
Zech	Zechariah		
Mal	Malachi		

As we learn about the baptism of Jesus, we come to see how the Holy Spirit can teach us about opportunities and possibilities.

One beauty of the Bible is its similarity to the Holy Spirit. Both use multiple levels of information and communication to bring about our transformation. God wants to bless you and bring you peace and healing at many levels. You may not always be aware of all of them yet He wants to bless you on many levels and through many channels.

Jesus' baptism marked the formal beginning of his ministry. Jesus had left his home in Galilee to be transformed by the ritual of baptism. Leaving behind all that was customary and familiar—his family, his friends, his neighborhood, town and region—he left his past and headed for a new life. Jesus went to the Jordan River specifically to begin his ministry, seeking a deeper relationship with God through it.

To mark this beginning, Jesus chose baptism, a public ritual. Jesus knew that rituals and symbols are important to us—to mark passages, to start new lives, to signal change. Scripture says that Jesus went to the Jordan for baptism in order to fulfill all righteousness. He was modeling for us a way to begin our new lives of service. By being baptized, Jesus fulfilled even the symbol of righteousness. This cleansing immersion in water gave us a symbol of beginning anew. There are a lot of other rituals in our lives that mark the beginnings of new things. Sometimes these are outward gestures and sometimes it is simply a desire and a decision to be new and clean.

When we begin a new life in Christ, we, too, can leave the past behind. We can leave behind past sin and past (so-called) friends with whom we have sinned. We even leave behind old ways of thinking and old dreams. When we start a new life in Christ, we are accepting his word and his direction for our lives. We are saying that we want the old us to be dead and buried, and the new us to be raised with Christ. We are also saying that we accept Christ as our leader and that we want to do his bidding.

Do you want to get closer to God? Do you want to fulfill even the symbol of righteousness? Then you already are because your desire to want closeness with God is what it takes. Every time you repent and ask for forgiveness you, too, are fulfilling the symbol of righteousness. Every time you confess and believe you are forgiven because God says you are, you have become clean. Most of us have to make a commitment many more times than once. And we keep being forgiven. Forgiveness is the medicine we receive so that we can get better.

At the Jordan, John the Baptist exhibited humility when he said that he was not good enough to baptize Jesus. John was so aware of his own sin that he didn't believe he was worthy. Of course he wasn't worthy enough. None of us is. Yet if God gives you a task to accomplish then you have or will have the ability because it is God's ability to empower even the weakest of us. Our inability magnifies God's ability.

At the same time, John was doing something else that was very right. He was looking to God for his sense of belonging and value. He demonstrated his willingness to look for God's direction, even if it differed from his own logic and sense of direction. One of the surest signs of your faith is your willingness to consider that your old ways were not working and that you are willing to learn new ways of thinking.

Jesus' answer to John says a great deal. He said, "Let it be so now, for it is fitting for us to fulfill all righteousness." He included John because of John's desire to do good. Jesus includes us even when we know we have no claim. It is our desire to do good that is so acceptable. None of us can reach that state of goodness by ourselves but we are responsible for what we let ourselves desire. Your very desire to do good and to become a better person through your faith in Jesus is where your righteousness comes from.

Jesus is called God's beloved son. Do you want that type of acceptance? Do you want to be told you are the beloved son or daughter in whom God is well pleased? To receive blessings and ultimate approval, God's approval, is wonderful. Evil knows how powerful is the person whom God blesses. Evil seeks to steal your blessings at every opportunity. Evil knows that God wants to bless us and to be close to us and wants to do for us. Evil also knows that if you receive those blessings, you will be stronger and a more purposeful witness for God even if you never open your mouth. The more that you allow God to bless you, the more powerful a witness you become to any and to all who see and who sense that you are different.

It is my prayer that today each of us begins anew and that we can become cleansed. I also pray that we are able to change what we can and allow God to change what we cannot. Amen.

How about starting the rest of your life with praise? You can, you know. Whether you are starting the rest of your life or the rest in your life, praise is a perfect way to begin.

Today may bring no glamorous or dramatic events your way. Many of our days—as well as many passages of the Bible—are like that. At first glance we might even overlook them. Such is the case with Luke 2:12-24. This passage documents a common religious practice in the life of every Jewish male. It is a ceremony that is done out of parents' obligation to their faith. Verse 21 reads, "After eight days had passed, it was time to circumcise the child; and he was called Jesus, the name given by the angel before he was conceived in the womb." Sometimes the ritual of the everyday can be life-changing if we allow it.

Circumcision was always performed as a symbol of the covenant between Abraham and God. Genesis 17 describes where the childless Abram makes a covenant with God. God tells him he will be made into the father of many people. At the covenant Abram becomes Abraham and Sari becomes Sarah. Circumcision was to be an everlasting sign in the flesh of the covenant.

Because Jewish law forbids mutilating the body, this is indeed a very special symbol. Before the covenant, Abraham and Sarah had been childless. We see the special and appropriate nature of this symbol when we realize the child Isaac was born because of God's gift and not of Abraham or Sarah's human ability. Sarah was far too old to have a child, yet through God's ability, she did.

All of our faith is based on the same concept: that God chooses to show Himself at times through the improbable and the impossible. It may be that circumcision is for men because they need more reminders than women do of who they are in relation to God. A child is Jewish if the mother is Jewish, because the mother's faith is so important to the development of the child's faith. Even if the father was a rabbi, unless the child's mother was Jewish, the child would have to convert. That is how important the mother is in passing on faith.

Jewish parents who were obedient to Jewish law realized this ceremony of circumcision was important. It is such an important celebration that it takes precedence over another commandment, the commandment not to work on the Sabbath. It takes precedence over any other holiday. It is important because the reminder of the covenant is so important. God promised to bless all the people of the earth through Abraham's seed. Like other rituals, on the surface as a physical act, it may or may not have any value. But as a symbol of tradition, it has much value.

Tradition has given us many ways in which we are blessed. Is it any wonder that people who have traditions and rituals tend to be healthier than people who don't? Traditions and rituals tend to remind us of who we are and to give us bearings. In a similar way, praise that we give to God also makes the day special and helps us to know who we are. By following traditions that are important to our faith, we remind ourselves who we are. When we add to that praise, we can really begin to add rest to the rest of our lives. Rest comes best when we feel that we are doing those things that we believe we are called to do, and when we let ourselves recognize our "specialness" in God's eyes.

Ceremony and tradition are helpful reminders of important things in our lives. Even everyday rituals of living are important when they bring us closer to God. It is our emotions—the flesh—from where temptation comes. Our emotions are not bad, even the ones that seem bad or are labeled as bad. But acting on our emotions as if they are compasses is no more logical than trying to drive in a certain direction by looking at the gas gauge. Using our emotions as indicator lights or gauges on the dash panel is much more helpful. Use your faith and its attendant traditions and rituals as your compass. The traditions of your faith remind you of the person you are. You can be in charge of your emotions and will feel good about yourself for having achieved this milestone of self-mastery through the ritual of the everyday awareness of who you are in relation to God.

It is my prayer that we all become more able to sense the presence of God in such a powerful way that we will want to call on Him in times of distress and temptation, and that we can praise Him more and more as we sense His love for us. Amen.

Before we can get forgiveness we have to receive confession.

One central theme of this passage is summed up by a verse in Isaiah 61:1 " . . . to proclaim the year of the Lord's favor, and the day of vengeance of our God. . . ." In the same breath are favor and vengeance, forgiveness and condemnation, pardon and accusation. One reason for these pairings is to emphasize their differences and to emphasize the importance of the difference. Also, it is to emphasize the fact that these things are all connected: God's favor, vengeance, condemnation, pardon and accusation all speak about our relationship with God.

Central to maintaining our relationship with God are truth and honesty, the same things that are required in any other relationship. Truth and honesty. They are central to any positive relationship. That is part of the reason that repentance and confession are so important to maintaining our relationship with God and to receiving the blessings that are offered.

If we have betrayed a friend, we need to confess, to repent, to want to repair the harm done and to repair the relationship. The same is true of our relationship with God. God will continue to forgive us, as long as we are willing to repent and to admit our mistakes. Admitting our mistakes isn't for God. It is for us. God can't possibly need our confession. *We do.* One of the only ways we can repair the damage done to our trust of ourselves or to our capacity for experiencing God's forgiveness is to confess and to repent. To not do so condemns us to bad feelings, and then we would attempt to deny our actions, to attempt to blot them out with some form of distraction, or to contribute to some powerful drama that brings bad feelings.

Jesus' first words of preaching are recorded as, "Repent and believe, for the Kingdom of Heaven is at hand." He skipped over a lot of preliminaries and got right to the important stuff! Repent and believe. To believe means to be willing to repent. Believing, in a matter of speaking, is repenting. All of us will sin. Even when we have made the most lasting and dramatic commitment to God, we will still sin. What really differentiates us as believers from non-believers is that we repent. Notice that Jesus begins his ministry with what will be a way to improve and deepen your relationship to God. That is because the most important thing we do is improve our relationship with God. The most important thing of all others. Our view of God impacts everything that we do or say whether we realize it or not. When you can envision God as loving you and caring about you, your world changes completely. Repentance is more than "I'm sorry." It is more than a half-hearted commitment, something you feel only partly like doing right now. It is more than a guilty feeling. It is more than being sorry that you were caught. Real repentance means that we recognize how important God is in our lives. We want God more than we want what we sinned about. Whether we are able to resist temptation that particular time or not, we are saying, "I want to restore my relationship with you, God."

Repentance is required because that willingness to want God in your life is what restores your relationship to God. Anything less and you wouldn't get your relationship restored. Some people fool themselves by becoming self-righteous but when you really want a good relationship with God, that desire becomes the thing that directs your course. What we get in return is forgiveness and restoration to a right relationship with God.

It is my prayer that we will continue to repent so that we will reap the blessings that God wants to give us. I pray that better still, we will reap the assurance of that satisfying relationship with God that passes all understanding. Amen.

Choosing Good Teachers
Jn 1:35-42

We sometimes think of a call occurring once. Yet we continue to be called, encouraged and led if we are willing to hear the Lord speaking to us.

This passage begins with some new knowledge and some implied wisdom. The day after Jesus' baptism, John the Baptist was standing with two of his disciples. (John had disciples, people who followed him in an effort to learn more about him and his teachings.) In Jesus' day, as today, people who wanted to learn something sought out and connected with people who had that special knowledge. This is true in professional development. It is true with developing a better understanding of the Bible. It is true with being close to God. We can seek knowledge and support from those who are already where we want to go.

When we have an image of someone doing what we want to achieve and when we look up to someone, we have an image of how we want to develop. We can model ourselves from their knowledge. I have used this approach throughout my life. I have people I admire who teach me about the Bible, about therapy, about health, about being close to God, about worship. Many of you have used this approach, too. Whether it is a teacher or a close friend, a person we spend time with will influence us.

John the Baptist told his disciples, "Behold the Lamb of God." Real teachers, the best ones, will point toward the Lamb of God. They will follow God in their own way. They will also teach us about following God. People who want us to follow them or some teaching that isn't the Lord's are just the blind leading the blind. Jesus is our Shepherd because he is the Lamb of God. Jesus is the Light.

The best teacher is one who can follow as well as lead. Jesus is the Lamb of God because he followed what God was directing him to do. He wasn't following his own whims. He was following what God told him to do. Whether at work, in our free time, in church or other places, we follow Him best when we surround ourselves with others who also are trying to follow Him. Two of John the Baptist's followers heard John call Jesus the Lamb of God and followed Jesus. This is right for us to do. We are to learn from others as they teach us to follow the Lord.

In this passage, we're instructed to realize that we are to shun immorality, and that we are to seek people to follow and learn from who shun immorality. When we do this and when we walk with the Lord, our walk becomes easier. There are many people whose dedication to the Lord, whose genuineness and sincerity and faith is inspiring. There are people who are letting the Lord lead them to emotional and mental healing. Some are truly letting the Lord lead them into sobriety. A genuine recovery is not just being addiction-free; a real recovery is spiritual, lasting and meaningful.

When the disciples caught up with Jesus, he spoke to them and said, "What do you seek?" He still asks us what we really want, what we are seeking. What we really search for does have a way of finding us. What do you seek? Are you looking for praise, for popularity, for followers, for people to tell you what you want to hear? Or are you seeking Jesus the Christ? When we seek after another other than the Lord, we are penalized. The first penalty is the sin itself. Idolatry of any sort causes us pain and loss. When we seek Christ in others, we are following in the footsteps of Andrew, Samuel, Mary Magdalene and all the genuine Christians down through the years. Samuel, Andrew, Peter, Paul and all of us who are truly seeking the Lord do so by learning what we can from people we admire for their faith, their knowledge and their walk with the Lord. As Christians we are to learn from each other. We are to help each other.

It is my prayer that each of us will rededicate ourselves to finding Christ and to seeking God's will in our lives by seeking the instruction that we can receive from others. I pray that we can truly tell others to come and see that we are finding Christ in each other. Praise God for His goodness in helping us to change and grow. Thank God for opening our eyes and senses. Amen.

You Can Feel Forgiven
Mk 1: 14-23

God speaks to us personally.

Now after John was arrested, Jesus came into Galilee preaching the Gospel of God. Jesus came bringing the message personally. It can be a comforting thought to know that God still uses the same method that He used then. When we listen to sermons, we are doing the same thing that people did 2000 years ago. God still speaks to us through sermons, perhaps because the Holy Spirit can mold and shape what we hear individually. One of the things that I like about preaching is the way the Holy Spirit works on me first, before I give a sermon. I like what it does to me because the Lord through the text speaks to me. Sometimes this is very powerful, showing me something I needed to see. And at other times, it is just very encouraging that God cares enough to correct me.

When he preached, Jesus wasn't trying only to reach people who needed physical healing. He was interested in reaching those people who needed healing in body, mind and spirit. He is still interested in reaching those who need hope, comfort, consolation and healing. He knows that we all need to be fed spiritually.

Jesus came preaching the gospel, saying, "The time is fulfilled and the kingdom of God has come near; repent and believe in the good news." Jesus came preaching the good and the new—God's good news. Being close to God and hearing a personal word is good news for us. Jesus said, " . . . the kingdom of God has come near . . ." meaning right now, here in the present. The kingdom of God is always at hand when we desire to be close to God in the present, right now.

And Jesus said, " . . . repent and believe . . ." Sin blocks us from getting closer to God. Sin blocks our relationship with truth. Sin refuses to hear truth, and when it hears it, it dismisses it. Our sin allows truth to be smothered quickly by urges and feelings that propel us to sin more and move toward more bad feelings. We can only believe when we repent. No repentance means no movement toward truth and no real belief. With no real belief, there's no real repentance. It's when we cut the ties to our sinful pasts that we are able truly to repent and believe.

We believers know only too well the real meaning of the word repent, to hate our past sin. We hate that we ever did those things. We have shame about having done them and wish that we could totally forget them. But Jesus had a better way. Those sins can be transformed from what dragged you down and caused you shame into what God has delivered you from. Most of us know intimately how our belief began—or began again—when we repented. And beyond the immediacy of repentance is that confessed sins can become the building blocks of even greater belief. Just as Jesus said of the woman who loves much because she is forgiven much, our forgiven sin can propel us to love much, to believe more deeply. What is worst about us can make us the best! Now that is good news.

Passing along the Sea of Galilee, Jesus saw Simon and Andrew. He saw the person Simon. He saw the person Andrew. He knew who they were. Jesus still sees the person. He sees you, the real you, the person who longs to be loved and accepted, the person who is hurt and frightened. The person who braves truth and is willing to let go of masks. Jesus saw Simon and Andrew casting fishing nets and he said, "Follow me and I will make you fishers of people." I love these verses. Jesus transformed Simon and Andrew from what they were to what they could become. Look at Matthew. He was a tax collector, in those days what we might think of as a legalized thief. Yet the Gospel of Matthew is the first in the Bible. Matthew had been someone who was despised yet he became well-liked and respected.

When we are willing to follow the call, to follow Jesus just as Simon and Andrew did, as James and John did, no matter what we have been, we can be transformed. They left what they were doing and followed him. So can we. Then there are greater blessings for us and for others. If we were people who hated, we can become people who love. He can transform us from our worst to His best.

It is my prayer that we can recognize that He is here with us, whether it is in a chapel or a cell. I pray that we recognize that He wants to free us so we can feel the good news and speak about it to others. I pray especially that we allow Him to guide and direct our steps into righteousness, and that when we let Him, our cups overfloweth. Amen.

When we place God in our lives and devote ourselves to Him, we can receive a clean spirit.

This passage is a continuation of the call of the disciples. "They went to Capernaum; and the sabbath came, he entered the synagogue and taught." Jesus began his ministry with his disciples in Capernaum, a city with a reputation for being a very sin-filled place. It would compare to some of our cities or parts of cities that are filled with drug trafficking, prostitution and the fencing of stolen goods.

"They were astounded at this teaching, for he taught them as one having authority and not as the scribes." We don't know if it was the people of Capernaum who were astonished or if it was the disciples or both. Jesus spoke here with authority about what is right and what is wrong. When we are most in sin, we want some definite answers. We want to have something we can count on. Sinful culture will always try to blur the distinction between right and wrong, between what sin is and what it isn't. But the Bible hasn't changed. What was sin is sin still.

"Just then there was in their synagogue a man with an unclean spirit." Some people have read this to indicate that people then believed in demon possession. Literally, the words refer to someone who has disregarded the laws of cleanliness. In Jewish tradition, there are many laws about how and how often to bathe, laws that show respect for God and for God's meetinghouse. The laws about cleanliness were to make a distinction between what was holy and what wasn't, between what was sacred and what wasn't.

We can be arrogant and laugh at the idea that people then believed in demon possession, though we may not know what they meant by that idea. Who among us, though, can say that when we have done wrong it did not feel like someone else was leading us? Who can honestly say that it never felt like a force was urging us to do wrong? Isn't an addiction like this? Sane people in their right minds do not throw away everything they have worked for a brief feeling. Isn't this a form of possession? It might be drugs. Or there are relationship addicts who allow another person to tell them where to go and what to do. Isn't this a kind of possession that steals our self and our courage? What's the difference, really, if we call it possession or addiction? When we have been so possessed with addiction that we allow ourselves to be humiliated, hurt and used for our fix—of a person, a drug or a feeling—we have not been in our right mind.

The ritual laws of cleanliness were to separate and keep pure that which was holy. We are to be holy. To be holy means to set aside unholy acts. Aren't addictions like this? Unfortunately, in this country, we have blurred many of the distinctions between what is holy and what isn't. We don't have a day for worship that is sacred and set aside from the others. Many of us haven't even set aside a time that is sacred for worship. It's important that we acknowledge God in special ways. Having a sacred time that we don't contaminate with sin is important.

"I know who you are! cried the unclean spirit." Evil always knows who Jesus is and whom he is with. Jesus commands the unclean spirit out of the man. He still commands the unclean spirit out of our lives. When we place God in our lives and devote ourselves to Him, we receive a clean spirit. Jesus helps us to have that clean heart and spirit. The command Jesus gave was "Be silent! And come out of him." When we sit silently with our God, much that is ugly leaves our lives because it means we are setting aside those moments to be with the Lord. The rest and peace we can receive then are better than the peace the world promises. Jesus is our preacher, teacher, doctor, lawyer, sister and brother. When we place him first in our lives, all else seems to go better.

Communion is about being made clean again. Confession and asking for forgiveness are daily ways we can be restored to spiritual health. Other ways are keeping a set time to read or pray or be silent, waiting for the Lord and dwelling on His Words.

It is my prayer that each of us would more fully receive the blessings that the Lord wants to give us and that we would especially recognize how sacred our relationship to God really is, so that we can deepen it and contribute more to improving it. Amen.

The Beauty Of Healing
Mk 1:29-39

Are you healing or are you hiding?

"As soon as they left the synagogue, they entered the house of Simon and Andrew, with James and John." If we look back at the verses preceding this one, we see that the party first went to Capernaum, immediately entered a synagogue, and then again immediately went to Simon's house. There wasn't any time for Simon to alert his wife or his mother-in-law that he would be bringing guests with him from his journey, and that one of them would be a famous preacher.

Simon Peter's (or Peter, as Simon becomes known as a disciple) impulsiveness is legendary. And yet when our impulsiveness is to the Lord, it is a good thing. Simon Peter is so excited about Jesus that he focuses entirely on getting the other people he loves to meet him. When we are first getting to know Jesus, we too may be so excited to know him that we want to introduce everybody to him. Like Simon Peter, we are so happy that we can be loved that we overflow with wanting others to experience this joy.

Of course, Simon Peter's wife may have felt embarrassment, fear, concern and perhaps anger when her husband arrived from his journey with guests. But when Jesus took her fevered mother's hand and healed her, no doubt her emotions changed to awe, appreciation, admiration and perhaps shock. When we bring Jesus home in our hearts to our loved ones, they receive blessings—and so do we.

Word of Jesus' healing quickly spread around Simon and Andrew's community. People began to bring their sick family members to Jesus. Many of us also are brought to Jesus or come ourselves because of an illness. Just like Simon and Andrew's neighbors, most of us came to Jesus when we were hurting, lonely, scared and sick. We needed healing for ourselves or for someone we love. We needed hope. We needed to be healed from the sickness of sin.

Quickly, Simon and Andrew's whole community knew that they followed Jesus. Talk about coming out of the closet with your faith! Everyone knew they were Christians. Does everyone know you are a Christian? Or are you being a secret agent?

When we are serious about following Jesus, things begin to happen that create new options for us. Simon Peter's wife and mother-in-law became believers and supported him. It seems like that is true for us. When we are on fire for the Lord, other believers notice and want us to succeed. They seem genuinely to want what is best for us. It is so different from being surrounded by envy, jealousy and bitterness.

Evil, of course, wants to use us. It may try to masquerade dependency as love. Sometimes we have been so desperate we fell for it. The intent by another person to use us may have been said as "I love you." And evil doesn't use just evil people to carry messages. Evil tricks decent people. They are fooled by evil's trickery. They don't have the ability to see their own neediness and how it is being exploited by evil. We make mistakes when we make decisions out of fear. On the other hand, when we operate from faith rather than fear, we usually choose pretty well. We make good decisions.

We get bombarded with strong emotions throughout the course of a day: fear, anger, temptation, denial, shame, envy, bitterness and grief. How do we really let go of these feelings so that we can start the next day with a clean slate? How do we close out today without going to bed contaminated with the day's emotions? The answer is in prayer, in time alone with God. Prayer helps us to clean out, start over and feel refreshed. Through prayer we get a renewed spirit. As great as Jesus' faith was, he, too, needed time alone with God. "In the morning, while it was still very dark, he got up and went out to a deserted place, and there he prayed."

Real love wants only what is good for us. When we place our trust in God, our entire orientation begins to change.

It is my prayer that each of us becomes such a prayer-dependent person that we allow our fever of sin to be released from our lives. I pray that we learn to depend heavily on God and that we are each able to receive the blessings He wants to give us. Amen.

Using 40 Days Well
Mk 1:12-15

"40 days" is real, symbolic and important.

We read, "And the Spirit immediately drove him out into the wilderness." Just after John baptized Jesus in the Jordan River, the Spirit of the Lord descended on Jesus and said, "You are my Son, the Beloved; with you I am well pleased." Can you imagine? There is no Academy Award, Nobel Prize or Pulitzer Prize, no earthly certificate or award that compares to the God of the universe declaring you to be His child, loved and favored. Jesus had just received the highest acknowledgement possible. His baptism, like ours, had begun his formal time of service to the Lord. Our baptism, like his, is our formal beginning as sons and daughters of God.

We are told in the first line of this passage a truth that all of us know. When you announce that you are going to follow the Lord or begin a deeper walk with God, the trials begin. "And the Spirit immediately drove him out into the wilderness." It seems that when we mark the beginning of our service to God with baptism, or when we start a commitment to the Lord, or when we give up a sin, we are immediately hit with temptation. The temptation or test or trial comes right after we have received some blessing. If evil can demoralize us or trick us into questioning the Lord's affection for us, then our blessing can be stolen.

Sometimes the trial happens right before we would be blessed if we continued to walk with the Lord. Evil wants to rob us of what we will receive. We could view a temptation as a reminder that we are about to be blessed. God wants us to see this because it implies faith.

The Spirit drove Jesus into the wilderness. The Spirit knew that temptation was coming and was preparing him for it. Being in the wilderness is preparation for what is to come. It is in the wilderness that the Hebrew children became a distinct people. Moses received the Ten Commandments in the desert. It is a place we all face in order to deepen our faith, to develop our confidence as Christians and to rely more deeply on the Lord. Being in the wilderness is so important for us Christians that immediately after being baptized, Jesus was driven into the wilderness.

Of course, in the wilderness there is hunger and thirst. These are powerful urges we feel that we must obey. During this time, we may feel that we have little or no way to receive comfort. All temptation in the wilderness has the strength of hunger and thirst. Yet when we resist temptation, it gets smaller, less powerful, less intense and less frightening. Eventually, as we continue to resist temptation, it leaves. We develop more and more confidence in the Lord. Our self-esteem begins to rise. Sometimes people want a magic wand with which to raise their self-esteem. They want things they can tell themselves so they will feel better. Real self-esteem comes as we allow the Lord to help us. We realize we have a friend who is always with us.

Jesus was in the wilderness for 40 days, tempted by Satan and with the wild beasts. There are struggles in the wilderness. Many of the people around you will be of no more help than wild animals. Not everyone we meet in the wilderness is an angel sent to help us! In the wilderness, the people around you can't help because it is your loneliness, your addiction or your temptation. In the wilderness, we also struggle with who or what we will worship. In Matthew, we are told that Satan tried to get Jesus to worship him. What is the struggle in your life?

Moses stayed on the mountain 40 days and 40 nights. Jesus stayed in the desert 40 days. It is in the wilderness that we have the opportunity to receive God's commandments inside of us. This is part of how we resist temptation, by welcoming, accepting and affirming our faith in God. When we face our loneliness and resist temptation, we are affirming who we are and what we want to be. As we struggle with our temptations just as Jesus did, God will send messengers to us to minister to us, even when we thought that no one was there or could be there for us. God sees what we do and He blesses us with comfort when we resist temptation. When we are in the wilderness, we can look for God's messengers to be there. They will be.

It is my prayer that each of us would begin to hear and realize that God already has said, "You are my beloved, in whom I am well pleased." I pray that we allow ourselves to rely on God so much that we receive blessings until our cup overflows and we know that even in the valley of the shadow of death, His rod and His staff comfort us. I pray that we know that He leads us out of the wilderness of the desert into paths of righteousness and to green pastures. Amen.

Faith Gives You New Eyes
                         Mk 9: 1-9

We can take the mountaintop with us into the valleys.

We have all had what I call "mountaintop experiences," experiences that
we will never forget, that touched us deeply and helped us to see a
situation in a radically new and different way. We all have mountaintop
experiences in our faith. By studying this passage in the context of what
comes before it, we can better understand how.

Jesus taught us that whosoever would lose his or her life for his sake and
for the sake of the Gospels will save it. This is the passage where Jesus
tells his disciples that he must go to the cross and, if they are to follow
him, they, too, must pick up their crosses. It is in this light that he
reassures them that some of them would not taste death before they see
the kingdom of God come with power. So the disciples know that Jesus is
going to the cross and they must follow. It puts intensity in the whole idea
of serving, doesn't it? For Jesus, it would lead to his death, a fact he faced
by relying on his faith

The disciples were told that they had to take up their crosses and follow
him. Picking up your cross means that you are willing to serve the Lord
through the circumstances to which He leads you. It means giving up our
prized idolatry, perhaps a prideful ambition, a fantasy, or something we
have longed for deeply. The irony is that when we are willing to sacrifice
our prized idolatry, just like Abraham on the mountain, we are spared from
losing it and are blessed. The moment when Isaac was spared was a
transforming experience for Abraham. He had many transforming
experiences just as you and I have had.

Transformation occurs when we interpret our lives through faith, when we
give up the world's perspective and use our faith instead. When we see
through our faith, our lives look different. As you change, your family and
friends will see you differently. They will be touched when they see your
faith and encounter your peace. It will give them hope and courage. Oh,
there will be some people who will try to belittle you and tear you down,
but these people are not from God. What can we expect from evil but
blame, deceit, sickness and death? If God has blessed you, He also has
hope that you will be a blessing to others. It may be that your
transformation to a person of faith will touch a number of people and give
you the opportunity to do something meaningful with your life.

Like Abraham, it is when we face difficult tests that we have the
opportunity for a mountaintop experience. Facing a difficulty, a crisis or a
temptation is a forerunner to a mountaintop experience. Sometimes we

face difficulties after a mountaintop experience. We are tempted to downplay the significance of the experience. Evil wants to belittle these events in your life where you know that God touched you, where He touched you and deeply affirmed your faith, where He helped you realize that you are cared for and about by a God who loves you and wants only good for you.

On the mountain, faced with something difficult, Peter blurted out whatever came to him. He spoke out of his fear, allowing it to control him. Peter is a good example for us: In spite of making this mistake, he continued. This is faith. Peter made the same mistake we might make and we, too, can rely on our faith and move forward.

This moment on the mountain was an event on which all believers can reflect. We can use our mountaintop experiences to inform, remind and continue to transform us during our everyday, ordinary times off of the mountain, when we are in the valley.

I knew a woman who could not feel good when she prayed. She felt guilty and did not feel the closeness to God that she wanted to feel and that she could feel. I taught her to pray using her mountaintop experiences, a technique from the Bible and from Jewish tradition. I said to her, "Think of a time when you know God was with you and when you felt blessed. Go ahead and recall that feeling. Now think of something from today for which you can be thankful to God." She grinned. She realized that she could get close to God by recalling those events and using them as a springboard. Psalm 100 says, "Enter his gates with thanksgiving and his courts with praise." When we are thankful and full of praise it changes us. It puts us in a mental position where we can encounter God. It is when we can experience God's presence. God doesn't need our thanksgiving and praise. We do! It transforms us. Instead of asking God for what we want, we thank God for what He is doing and has done for us.

It is my prayer that you are able to know that it is my hope that these words provide you with comfort, and that you are able sense God's caring for you this day and everyday. Amen.

In spirit and in truth . . .

Just before this passage, Jesus had spoken to the Samaritan woman in a direct manner. He saw her sin and continued to accept her. This is a freeing experience for any of us. Admitting your mistakes to yourself, to God and to one other person who continues to accept you is an important step. It is freeing because it means we can stop pretending, hiding and being afraid. At least one person knows the worst about us and still accepts us.

Moving toward this can help give you the faith and courage to break evil's hold on you. Confessing our sin is a way of stopping the continued cycle of emotional abuse that secrecy perpetuates. We can begin to feel better and start to respect ourselves again. A full confession, where we accept responsibility, frees us more fully. A partial confession gives us only partial relief.

The woman with whom Jesus spoke seemed to have gotten relief from her emotional pain. As a result, she could talk with Jesus about worship. Talking about how we pray or how we worship is risky; it can make us feel vulnerable. It can be very intimate. Once the shame with which evil controls us is gone, though, we are freer to focus on the things we want to focus on. Shame is like insulation that keeps us from hearing God's Word. Sin separates us from God, others and ourselves. The woman with whom Jesus spoke at the well was isolated from her townspeople. Yet after this encounter with Jesus, she ran back to her community. She was excited that she could hold her head up. She could look people in the eyes and feel good about herself. Jesus knew that by helping her to confess, she would feel cleansed and able to reconnect with herself, God and others.

Jesus and the woman discussed worship. In their day, there was controversy over where to worship. Jesus told her something timeless and useful for us to recognize. He said that true worshippers worship the Father in spirit and in truth. We could study this sentence for days or weeks, because it is filled with meaning. "In spirit and in truth."

What does this mean, to worship God in spirit? Are we to worship God as a spirit who is not in any one location? Yes, in part, though there is much more. It means also that we need to pay more attention to and have respect for the spiritual realm. So often, we get stuck in our material concerns and in thinking defined by our material world. In the spirit, God can listen to all of our individual prayers and be with us personally and privately. In the physical world, that would be impossible. Distance and time would have no meaning to God as a Spirit.

We are to worship in spirit and in truth. This can mean that we need to be in the spirit to worship God in spirit. In part, this means that we are to focus on and think about spiritual things rather than material things, a task much easier said than done! Worshipping in spirit means seeing the spiritual realm even in the material world. In part, it means putting our faith into practice. It means looking for opportunities to see, hear and react to this world from the spirit, from a place of faith. For example, it might mean looking for how God is seeking to bless us even though we did not get what we wanted in a particular situation.

Worship in spirit means looking for God's presence in prayer. It means living like we have been cleansed and forgiven after communion. It means studying His Word. It means looking for His spirit in everyday life so we can know how to recognize and find him today.

There are also multiple layers of meaning in the phrase "worshipping in truth." When you worship in truth, you recognize God's Spirit in all truth. You can look for God's presence and meaning in all truth. God's truth is everywhere and God is in truth. We cannot worship God with a false heart. We can't worship the God of truth and be about lies or living a life of deception, secrecy or even shame. We can value truth so highly that we tell the truth as best we can with all people. We can all let go of the petty disagreements about material things. Truth is spiritual and connected to our real worship, our true sense of self. If you want self-esteem, always tell the truth and clear up lies you have told. Your spirit will soar and so will your self-esteem.

Confession relieves us of the responsibility to cover up the truth. Are you willing for everyone to know what you do in secret? How highly you hold the truth speaks volumes about you. Who do you think knows the answers? We may find that often, confession is our acknowledgement of what everybody else knew all along!

It is my prayer that you are able to receive fully that clean knowledge that comes from confession and forgiveness. I pray also that whether you are able to participate physically in communion or not, you will receive its spiritual blessings. Amen.

From bitterness to calm, from hate to forgiveness, from jealousy to joy . . .

The verse contained in this passage is the most quoted and best-known verse in the Bible. Many of us have strong feelings about this passage. Maybe you always understood it or perhaps it symbolized something good and accepting to you. Perhaps today it means something even more powerful for you. You may have a smile on your face as you quote it. The rest of the passage also has much to teach us.

Verse 14 reads, "And just as Moses lifted up the serpent in the wilderness, so must the Son of Man be lifted up." You may remember when Moses and the Hebrew people were in the wilderness, there came a time when they refused to listen to the Lord. Poisonous snakes came around them and many people were being bitten and were dying. Moses asked God what could be done. God told Moses to make a staff with a serpent attached to the top. Those who saw the symbol and became believers lived. They believed God's promise that seeing the symbol would let them live even if a snake bit them. This remains a strong symbol today, used by the American Medical Association to mark doctors' offices and hospitals, places where people go looking for healing. Do you suppose the AMA realizes it is telling people that God's Word still heals us?

In this passage, the word *believe* is important. We may already believe. But if we don't, how do we begin? If we struggle with how to believe or whether to believe, how do we settle this inner strife?

The word *believe* means to think that something is true. In Greek, it means even more than this. It means to respond to an inner knowing of God's truth. *To believe* means to accept the truth that God placed inside of us as created human beings. To believe means to respond to the inner urging that tells us that God's Word is true. This is why you can feel calm when you accept God's truth. You can relax and let go of the tension and struggle in your life. Not believing means ignoring the truth that God created us with an inner knowing inside of us. It's like a bird flying north, east or west for the winter instead of south. We really do have the instinct for taking the right direction in our journeys.

This passage is about good and evil, the two sides. Matthew 7:21 quotes Jesus as saying, "Not everyone who says to me, 'Lord, Lord,' will enter the kingdom of heaven, but only the one who does the will of my Father in heaven." In other words, there is no meaning in just mouthing the words but not living them. Belief means putting into practice what we believe. We cannot fool God. We may fool some of the people around us and ourselves, but God knows the truth even if we don't. Jesus said that when we do the will of the Father, our belief shows. He also said that those who follow His commandments love Him. If we love Him, we will want to follow His Word. It shows in our actions. It shows in our emotions. It shows in how we treat others. We begin to want to follow His commandments. We may struggle but we want to follow them. Our emotions change from bitterness to calm, from hate to forgiveness, from jealousy to joy.

Everyone who does evil hates the Light and does not come to the Light lest their deeds be exposed. Proverbs tells us both to correct non-believers and not to correct them. This translates into this: Correct them and they will only hate you. But we're to correct them so they will not think they are wise. When people are ignoring God, God's Word and the internal voice that tells us to believe in the Bible, they don't enjoy someone else telling them this. Essentially, we're to recognize when someone is following evil and then demonstrate our own belief—not with arrogance but with quiet wisdom. It may show in how respectfully we treat the Word of God. It shows in how we treat others. It is clear that God is present in the deeds of the person who does what is true and who comes to the Light.

Real belief includes seeking instruction so that we may eliminate more sin from our lives. Running from instruction shows a lack of belief. People show their hate for the Light by refusing to listen, by declaring wrong anyone who points out a flaw. Sometimes we refuse to recognize God speaking to us through others. We may do this repeatedly. This is evidence of sin, not of faith. The courage it takes to face our sins and to desire to do better—even over and over—demonstrates so much faith. God will deliver us from the struggle, especially as we get more of His Word into our hearts and minds. He knows when you are seeking to do His will even when you do not know how. Our God knows that you want more peace, more assurance of being accepted, loved and included with those whose sins are forgiven. It is really this simple: If you are striving to do God's will, then your sins are already forgiven. As you continue to act on your belief, and know and show that your sins are forgiven, even more signs of the Spirit will be with you.

It is my prayer that each of us can begin to be comforted by signs of our belief developing and growing. I especially pray that we allow God's gifts of peace, love, joy and comfort to live inside of us, and that we can feel His peace as a sense of calm. It may begin in our feet, just like when Jesus washed the disciples feet, or it may begin with our heads, like being anointed with oil, or it may just be a knowing that reassures us. Amen.

Letting God Help With Loneliness
Jn 12:20-33

We can choose loneliness and our way or the presence of God and His way.

Most of us have felt lonely at one time or another. Feeling that profound loneliness where no one seems to understand or listen to us is truly painful. Evil enjoys tricking people into that place because they are so vulnerable from such a place of such pain. Our God delights in delivering us from that place of loneliness and in restoring us.

In Jeremiah, God tells us that he will make a new covenant with his people, that He will put His law inside of us and write the covenant upon our hearts. So that from the least to the greatest of us can know Him, He tells us that He will forgive our inequity and remember our sins no more. The covenant that God wrote on our hearts urges all of us to know Him.

God's grace in forgiving us writes His law upon our hearts. We begin to want to keep His laws, not to avoid punishment but because we appreciate being forgiven and appreciate the peace this brings us. It is right that we dwell on God's forgiveness of us. It is right that we dwell on Him urging us to make decisions that bring us real peace and happiness

Jesus taught, "Very truly, I tell you, unless a grain of wheat falls into the earth and dies, it remains just a simple grain; but if it dies, it bears much fruit." There is a lot of meaning in this passage. Baptism is really first about our death. It is about our old self of sin dying and our new birth into God's family. By "dying" to ourselves and really accepting God into our lives, we are no longer alone. We have God's presence with us. One proof is the love, joy, peace, patience, kindness, generosity, faithfulness, gentleness and self-control that Gal 5:19 lists as the fruits of the Spirit. Few of us have all of these fruits yet if we have accepted God into our lives, we will evidence some of them.

So why do we feel so lonely at times? Why are there times when we can't sense God's presence? Some of the time, I can really sense Him. Other times, I can't really feel His presence and reassurance. One answer lies in sin. Sin blocks us from ourselves, from each other and from God. It's hard to see this sometimes. At times, sin masquerades as something else and it's only later that we realize we need to confess and be forgiven and restored to feel His presence.

Jesus taught us, "Those who love their life lose it, and those who hate their life in this world will keep it for eternal life." Our culture has so overused the word *love* that we are confused about who ought to be in charge of our lives. "Loving our life in the world" is our wanting control over our choices and what happens to others and us. On the surface, it looks good to be in control of our decisions and to want good things for others. What's wrong with that? Nothing, until what we think ought to happen become the only things we will accept. Then we have displaced God from our lives. Then our pride and our fear are ruling us, not our faith.

Often it is a mixture of both pride and fear that gets in our way and causes us to feel lonely. When we turn our worry and concern over to the Lord and let go, we feel His peace. When we turn it over to God we are saying in effect, "I'm open to your way, God, and your possibilities, and I realize I can't control much in my life except whether I will trust you or not."

We can begin healing only when we admit that our lives are unmanageable and that our choices without God's guidance have gotten us into trouble. Sometimes we may catch ourselves trying to take control back over and over. Each time, we can give control back to God and feel His presence. Proverbs 3: 5, 6 and 7 read: " Trust in the Lord with all your heart and do not rely on your own insight. In all your ways acknowledge him, and he will make straight your paths. Do not be wise in your own eyes, fear the Lord and turn away from evil." It is so neat that all we need to do is acknowledge God and His protection blesses us.

When we are trying to be in charge, we can't ever seem to fill up that emptiness, that loneliness. Deep down, we know that the only thing that really satisfies is putting our life and control in God's hands and living by His Word as our guide. No matter how strong our faith, sometimes we need to be reminded. And no matter how often we stray, He will gently urge us back. We all know that when we let Him, He leads us beside still waters and makes us to lie down in green pastures.

It is my prayer that each of us might begin to feel His hand on our shoulder, reassuring us and reminding us that He is with us. I pray that we can do this now or when we are praying alone or when we find ourselves feeling lonely. Then, like the psalmist, we can each say, "He restores my soul." Amen.

Humility Helps Us Change
Mk 11: 1-10

Blessed is he who comes in the name of the Lord.

This passage is referred to as the Triumphal Entry. It recounts Jesus' entry into Jerusalem before he was crucified, the manner of his entrance reflecting Zechariah's prophesy of how the Messiah would enter the city. Hundreds of years before, Zechariah (9: 9) said, "Lo, your king comes to you; triumphant and victorious is he, humble and riding on a donkey, on a colt, the foal of a donkey." He goes on to say that this King's empire will stretch from sea to sea and cover the entire Earth, and that he will set captives free to a new covenant.

It was not by accident that Jesus rode into Jerusalem on a donkey, the foal of an ass. To complete the prophesy of Zechariah, the Messiah had to come into the city in this humble manner. In ancient times the donkey was a sign of humility. So often, when an important person arrives in a city, there is much preparation and fanfare, lots of music and backslapping. How different was Jesus' arrival in Jerusalem, marked by humility, not by pride or prestige. How different. . . . and yet, this is how differently the world and the church see life.

Jesus did not have to fulfill this obscure ancient prophecy. He wanted to, to say to all that he was here to usher in a new covenant, a spiritual change so profound that no worldly fanfare could compare. Jesus wanted to fulfill the words of Scripture because he felt loved by God. He wanted to do for God because he was appreciative and thankful. And he wanted others to see the blessing that would come with his fulfilling of the prophecies.

The people lining the road the day Jesus rode into the Holy City were seeking the Messiah. They wanted to worship God, to praise Jesus and to celebrate his entrance into Jerusalem. Using the things that were available to them, they took up palm leaves to show respect for and to him as he passed by. This is why we celebrate Palm Sunday.

The people that day experienced something profound and special that stayed with them for the rest of their lives. At times you have been reading your Bible and you realize suddenly something you did not know before. At times you have been praying or attending service, and you suddenly feel close to God. You know that you are accepted and forgiven. It's not even a question. And you know that it is a special day. Perhaps you even have been realizing that you have been receiving it more and more, and are getting closer to God.

Jesus' entrance into Jerusalem on a borrowed donkey is as far as you can get from worldly success. This show of humility teaches us to be humble before God, and to rely on our humility to lean on and seek help from God. When we try to fulfill the requirements of the Bible out of a sense of duty, well, it's a difficult task. When addicts rely solely on their willpower so as not to abuse drugs, they'll have a very tough time over the long haul. When they admit their powerlessness and let God help, they not only succeed but also have an easier time during recovery.

The people along the road to Jerusalem said, "Blessed is he who comes in the name of the Lord." That has such a deep wisdom in it. To want to bless the person who comes to us in faith is both right and wise. The person who comes to us in the name of the Lord can more easily be believed and can be trusted. The people you can trust are those in whom you sense a deep and true sense of faith. When others really have the Spirit of the Lord, we can rejoice and be happy!

Of course, there are people who *say* they are faithful, who delude themselves about how much the Holy Spirit is in their lives. A good candidate for your trust is the person who is humble and seeks no fame, someone who wants to serve. But there must be even more evidence: that when you listen to the Holy Spirit inside of you, you are told that this is someone who can be trusted.

As Jesus approached Jerusalem, the fist thing he wanted to do was go to the temple. He received comfort there, and taught us that we, too, can seek comfort from God. That we want to receive a special closeness to God says something about us. When we want to do God's will and have Him be our teacher and friend, doctor and lawyer, it says something about us. It especially says something special about you when you seek closeness to God in the midst of doing other things. Just like the people along the road to Jerusalem, you spontaneously feel that you want to praise Him. That you want to be close to God and praise Him and serve Him says a lot about you. That you want your family to feel close to God and that you want them to understand how important God is to you is about your love for them and for God.

It is my prayer that over the next few days, each of us finds ourselves thinking spontaneously about and praising God. I thank God for you and your faith, and I pray that your friends and families are able to see your faith growing each and every day. Amen.

The Truth Can Heal And Transform You
                                Mk 16: 1-8

He restores my soul.

Today's passage records three women receiving the greatest honor that anyone could receive. On Easter morning, they were the first to the tomb where Jesus' body had been left. True to how Jesus treated women during his lifetime, it's fitting that three women were the first to witness the Resurrection. They were the first ministers to tell others that Jesus had been raised from the dead. They were the only ones to get the news from the angel. It is odd that even today, some people say that the only proof we have of Jesus' resurrection is an empty tomb. This is wrong. We also have the testimony of three women who were given this honor because of their honesty and devotion.

In Jesus' day, there was a great deal of prejudice against Samaritans, Gentiles and women. It took two male witnesses to declare anything. Women who declared that something had happened were not believed. So devalued was their word that women could not legally testify to anything. Though the ancient world may not have respected women, Jesus did. And God bestowed upon these three women the greatest honor anyone could receive.

Scripture says, "And when the sabbath was past," Mary Magdalene, Mary, the mother of James, and Salome brought spices with which to anoint Jesus' body. In the ancient world, people showed respect to the deceased by washing the person's body and anointing it with burial spices. Out of respect for God's laws, the women waited until the day after the Sabbath. This must have been very difficult for them but because of their devotion, they waited. They were rewarded for their willingness to be obedient and for their desire to serve.

Today, we are still rewarded. When we respect God's laws, we are blessed. When we break them, there is always a penalty. The commandments were God's protection to His chosen people. They were a way to reveal spiritual truths so that His chosen could be blessed and protected.

We can believe the story of the three women and the empty tomb because of the women's words, what the disciples saw, and because it is written in the Bible. Yet there is other proof, wonderful and amazing proof. It is in each of us, in our capacity to learn to see spiritual, moral truths. The truth feels different than a lie. The truth can heal. It can be counted on and built upon. The truth endures. How different this is from a lie, which has no energy of its own and must be refueled. When people live lies, everything around them is affected. The dishonesty steals their very ability to know the truth.

People who live the truth are also affected. They are blessed day in and day out. When Jesus was invited into your life, he began to change you in new ways. With Jesus in your life, you feel differently. You act differently. You feel peace and comfort. You may even have cried a lot because you were so grateful for the ways in which he is blessing you.

I think that there is proof of Easter in you. The proof is in the way you have changed. It is clear to anyone who is willing to see spiritual truths. You may have been healed of addictions. You may have been healed of bitterness and the shadow of shame from your past. You may have been healed of dishonesty. Some of you are being restored to honesty and to health. You can see it and you can sense it.

Jesus continues to change us and to bring us new life. I have seen bitterness replaced with peace and hatred replaced with love. I have seen hurts healed. Jesus changed my life and I know he continues to help me today. I know he continues to change you as well. God's grace is so awesome and powerful that truly, as the psalmist said, He restores my soul. He blesses us with a resurrection here today and now, and He gives us hope for the future

Easter marks Jesus' resurrection from the dead. There is no event in all of history that has been of more importance. There is no event in the future that will be as important until Jesus returns. This day, we can celebrate the fact that many people have discovered that Jesus was raised from the dead. We can rejoice that there is proof in you.

It is my prayer that each of us will become an even more powerful example of God's healing touch, so that like the first women who discovered Easter, each of us can tell others so they, too, will be transformed by Jesus' life and love. Amen.

Forgiveness Is Powerful Medicine
Lk 23:33

Depending on your point of view—sacred or secular—Good Friday will look different.

Jesus' journey to the cross was horribly intense. He had been beaten with men's fists and then whipped. The whip had bones tied into its lash so that it would tear his flesh. He had been gouged with a crown of thorns and emotionally humiliated. Already physically exhausted, he then was nailed to a cross. Crucifixion was designed to cause intense and searing pain as the nails hammered into hands and feet hit nerves.

It was in the midst of this kind of unimaginable pain that Jesus said, "Father, forgive them, for they know not what they do." In his agony, he prayed for the people who were abusing him! He prayed to God to forgive the soldiers who had nailed him to a cross. He prayed for the authorities that had judged him. He prayed for the people who watched so they could feel important later when they told the news to others.

None of the people there that day deserved to be forgiven. They were all doing evil intentionally. They were willingly and openly doing harm. The Roman soldiers did not deserve to be forgiven. They were using their power to cause the most pain they knew how to cause. They mocked Jesus and gambled for his clothes, using these arrogant behaviors to deny their guilt. Neither the judges nor the spectators deserved to be forgiven.

We do not feel that the self-righteous person who judges others while ignoring his or her own sin deserves to be forgiven. Really, these people deserved only blame and punishment. Yet, in his pain, Jesus prayed for them to be forgiven. Even though they had not earned it, he prayed for them anyway. Perhaps Jesus even allowed the pain to motivate his prayer for their forgiveness. Although it is difficult to do, prayer for others while we ourselves are being hurt is the most powerful way to cope with pain.

We may not like to believe this, but we are like those people in many ways. We have used power or knowledge to hurt others. We have said things that we knew brought hurt to someone, sometimes even to those whom we love. We all have stood by and watched silently while someone was being verbally assaulted. Perhaps we have allowed others to be abused or physically hurt in our presence. We have made fun of people, mocking them or scoffing at them. We may have tried to justify these things saying, "It was none of my business." Well, people have been shifting blame off of themselves from the time of Adam and Eve.

You might ask, "What if I am the one being mocked or abused? Am I more deserving of forgiveness?" But we have all sinned. Our roles are not what bring us forgiveness. Jesus' example that day tells us that God has set a very different requirement than "deserving."

To be forgiven, we must first acknowledge our sin. To be forgiven, we must acknowledge God and to do that we must also acknowledge that we have disobeyed and belittled God by our actions. For the perpetrators of evil on the day of the Crucifixion, the first step was up to them. By acknowledging their sin and God's presence, they could and would be forgiven.

All sin mocks God. All sin scoffs at God. Sin tells us to say, "I can do it myself!" Sin says that we are on a par with God. Sin insults the boundaries that God requires us to have toward each other, the Word, ourselves and to God. There is no amount of excuse or denial that justifies sin. Sin is sin. Even when we acknowledge it to God and are forgiven, its scar will remain upon our hearts. But with humility and an acknowledgement of what we have done, we are forgiven. God's forgiveness can restore us. It can give us the ability to do things differently. The shame of sin becomes the boast of God's power. Through God's forgiveness, we can let go of the shame and be able to be a witness to God's power to heal, to overcome.

Forgiveness was the most powerful way for Jesus to ease his pain that day. Holding onto anger or hurt, and refusing to forgive only hurts us. It traps us in a painful cycle. Jesus gave us a powerful example of how to treat others and ourselves. The prayer he taught us says it well. " . . . Forgive us our trespasses as we forgive those who trespass upon us . . ." (or: "Forgive us our debts as we forgive our debtors . . .") Forgiveness heals us. It is the most powerful medicine we have to heal our sin. The nature of sin is that once we commit a sin, we are drawn to commit more of it. Forgiveness breaks this cycle. We are forgiven and we, in turn, forgive.

It is my prayer that we receive even more of His offered forgiveness and begin to more fully feel its power to heal, restore and empower us. I especially pray that the people around you begin to recognize the change that God is working in you and bringing to completion until it is finished. Amen.

More important than whom you know is who knows you.

In this important and gentle passage, Jesus teaches us that he is the Good Shepherd. He is the one we are to follow. If we believe in him, invite him into our hearts, and want to follow him then we are his sheep. In verse 14, Jesus says, "I know my own and my own know me." If you want to know Jesus, you have already asked him into your life. You want to be directed by him. He is your Shepherd.

When he describes himself as the Good Shepherd, Jesus implies that there are other shepherds who are not good. They are pretenders. When you think about this, you know it is true. At one time or another, most of us have listened to other shepherds. Whether they were associated with a religion or not, they became our shepherds when we were willing to follow them. This might be a specific person or something else entirely; When a person's sense of their importance is derived from drugs, the "in" crowd, fashion, being popular, or something similar, then that person is worshipping these other things and has chosen another shepherd.

Jesus contrasts the Good Shepherd with a hireling, someone who does not really care for the sheep but rather, is hired merely to tend them. If we were talking about religion, for example, a hireling might be a minister who really did not care about Jesus' sheep but was exploiting them for his or her own gain.

When we look back over our lives, at the times we were abandoned, hurt, left in trouble, or perhaps just depressed, we had been placing our trust in someone other than the Good Shepherd. No matter who they are, hirelings will let us down, either intentionally or simply because of life events. Every time we make someone other than Jesus our shepherd, it costs us dearly. Our dependency on other shepherds belittles us and ultimately hurts us in many ways, for anyone and anything except God will leave us. This is sin: when we listen to another's voice, when we reject God by placing someone or something above Him.

Sin often begins when we are tricked into believing that God is not here for us or that He is holding the good stuff out for someone else. This is just how evil operates: convincing us that its rewards are good for us. Evil tries to trick us. If we didn't think we would benefit from joining evil, who would ever be deceived? Sometimes, evil tricks us by telling us we will not feel guilty if we stop listening to God. Sometimes, evil tries to convince us that the hurt, anger and shame that we feel are God's fault, that because God did not stop certain things, God is responsible.

31

Who among us has not said, "How could a loving God let these things happen?" Who among us has not struggled with the fact that there is pain and suffering in the world? How could we read a newspaper and not be aware of the floods, earthquakes, fires and other natural disasters that occur? Or see the man-made disasters of pain and suffering brought on by cruelty or abandonment? And what about death?

There is pain and suffering in our world. God never promised that He would keep us free of these things. I suspect it would be impossible. To be alive is to experience pain and suffering. It is the way of the world. What Jesus does promise is that he will stay with us, that he will help us, that he will guide us, that he will protect us from the one who can steal our souls. Of course, I am speaking of evil. By exploiting the emptiness in our hearts, evil steals souls, sometimes over a long period of time.

We all have some of this emptiness, this void, a sense of worthlessness, helplessness and powerlessness that feels hopeless. Thank God that the Lord restores our souls. Most of us can bear witness to that. We have had our souls restored from the brink of hopeless despair. We have been hurt, abandoned, and led astray. Thank God He sought us out and restored us to our right minds and gave us back our sense of dignity, honor and respect. We keep safest by listening to God's voice.

How do we know, though, that it is truly His voice? If the same instruction, direction and purpose are taught to us in the Bible, then we can count on it. If not, the voice is not from God. God's truth is pure top to bottom, inside and out, through and through. The entire Bible is related to the rest of the Bible. We do best when we use one truth in the Bible to help us understand other truths there.

And how do we know if it is Jesus' voice interpreting Scripture or not? If we are sheep, we know his voice. We know his gentleness, love and care. He cares enough to tell us when we are wrong, though he delights in bringing us blessings. If you wonder about who is right about something, remember these words Jesus said. "I have other sheep that do not belong to this fold. I must bring them also, and they will listen to my voice." Whatever your denomination, there is one shepherd: the Good Shepherd. There is one flock, and it is all of us.

It is my prayer that each of us deepen our relationship with and our commitment to the Good Shepherd as He restores our souls, is with us even in the valley of the shadow of death, fills our cup to overflowing, anoints us for service, and leads us into paths of righteousness. Amen.

"No pain, no gain" applies to more than exercise.

Jesus' first words in this passage were, "Peace be with you." Jesus wanted his disciples to receive the peace that goes with knowing him. At first, though, the disciples were not able to feel this. They were startled and frightened. And, behind their fear, they doubted. Jesus asked them why. Why did these thoughts appear in their hearts?

Sometimes we doubt because there is so much fear and temptation in our lives. At the height of temptation, doubt seems to kick in and push us into sin. At the core of every sin is the feeling that we will not be all right if we don't get enough of some earthly person or thing. For example: "How will I ever be able to relax if I don't have that drink?" Doubt arises when we have taken our eyes and minds off of God, and, instead, are focused too much on our own condition. This is when we can begin to head toward sin, when we exclude God from our thinking. Instead, we can fill our minds with God's Word and keep our attention focused on His truth.

Doubt especially tends to creep in when we feel fear—fear of change, fear of loss, or fear of not being enough. Jesus responded to his disciples' fear by showing them his hands and feet. Inviting them to touch him and to watch him eat, he used everyday things to show them that he was real. He wanted them to focus on him in that moment to see the truth. This is an important lesson for us. We can focus on how we see God in any moment to break ourselves out of a trance of doubt or temptation. The more we are able to sense God's presence with us, the easier time we'll have.

Some people have said that in the face of being transformed into healthier people, they felt their fear and loneliness so intensely that they thought they were losing their minds. Perhaps they were! Hallelujah to losing a mindset that trapped and hurt us. Romans 12:2 reads, "Do not be conformed to this world, but be transformed by the renewal of your minds, that you may discern what is the will of God—what is good and acceptable and perfect."

We struggle, many of us, when we try to conform to the demands of the world and still keep our faith. It can indeed make a person feel as though he or she is losing his or her mind. The world's demands for conformity may encourage us to stay the way we are, even if we're unhappy or addicted. They may come from our families or from our own desires to be like others so they will like us. The disciples that day long ago were trying to fit what they were seeing into previous experiences and an old way of thinking. Our old ways of thinking might get in the way of our path to joy, too. But just as the disciples were transformed, we, too, can develop a new way of understanding ourselves, a healthier and more spiritual way.

We are told that Jesus opened the Scriptures to his disciples. Now these disciples had been with Jesus for three years. They had watched him preach and perform miracles. They probably could quote Scripture and some of things that Jesus had said. But Jesus had to open their minds to Scripture. How come? Because understanding Scripture does not come just from attending Bible study or listening to preaching. True understanding of Scripture comes from God. It is a gift through faith.

God gives us our understandings of the Bible. Sometimes these come as flashes of insight. Other times you will experience a growing awareness, thinking that evolves as you do. This is part of what makes God's Word exciting and alive. It changes as we do. As we are different next week or next year, if we are earnestly seeking God, His word will evolve with us. The Scriptures open to faith—and only to faith. Evil might try to trick us into its false interpretation of the Bible, but we can tell the difference when we see that the Bible is true at every level. It is in line with other parts of Scripture and promotes or agrees with our obeying God's directives.

Jesus told his disciples that it was in the Scriptures that he would suffer, die and then rise on the third day. He declared that repentance and forgiveness of sins is preached in his name for all nations. He told us that our sins can be washed completely away and through repentance, we can be forgiven. He was telling us that he will become our advocate and companion, and that he will take away our loneliness.

He said that day that the disciples were his witnesses to these things. We are still his witnesses. He said, "And see, I am sending upon you that which my Father promised; so stay in the city until you have been clothed with power from on high." Jesus' wisdom is timeless. When we try to do everything from our own power, how we can struggle. When we wait for power from God and move in God's time, how we can be centered and whole.

It is my prayer that each of us will wait on God's direction and power to come to us rather that trying to everything ourselves—including cleaning up our behavior—because through God's power, we can resist temptation. With God's power we know what to say and do. Amen.

What does abide mean?

Jesus used allegory and parable to say something not said as easily without these devices. He used them also to relate concepts to everyday life.

"I am the true vine and my Father is the vinegrower." This sentence implies that there are other vines that are false. In Greek, the word *true* means "the one and only." In ancient Rome, there were many religions, just as there are today. Ancient Rome encouraged people to think that each of these many religions was equal to all of the others. Jesus goes right to the core of this issue. He is the one and only true vine and God the Father is the vine grower. Eternity outlasts current vogues and political climates. Jesus is letting even us Christians know something profound, that he must be at the center of our religious lives; else we have been worshipping in vain.

Jesus is clear that branches with no fruit will be removed. If there is no evidence in our lives that what Jesus said has made a difference to us, there is no fruit. Jesus expects us to follow his teachings and to change our lives. We are either striving for closeness to him or we're not. There's no middle ground on this one. People who constantly and/or covertly refuse to give up their favorite sins and alter their lives will bear no fruit and their branches will be taken away. What happens to a vine with no branches?

For those of us who are seeking closeness to Jesus, our request will be granted. God the Father prunes our branches. Again, back to the Greek, the word *prune* means *to clean.* God will clean us. If we hold onto Jesus and are doing what we can to follow his words, God will clean us. He will take away the dead, useless and draining parts of our lives. Yet even more than cleansing sin from our lives, God honors our faith in Jesus by cleaning even our pasts. All of the things we did before—things that left us feeling dirty, soiled and unfit for God—God will clean. I thank God for being clean and for wiping out our past sins. He will do what we cannot. He will cleanse us and it will show in our lives.

In verses four and five, Jesus emphasizes the foundational truth that unless we abide in him, we produce no good fruit. Most of us are only too aware of the bad fruit, the sin that we produce on our own. Jesus says that apart from him, we can do nothing. Apart from him, only shame, destruction and ruin, and death can occur. Apart from him, people argue, fight and become bitter. They complain and form cliques and groups to bolster their sagging self-esteem. It is all in vain. Without Jesus, they can do nothing.

One way to tell if Jesus is part of someone's life is the evidence of the fruit. Is she bitter? Does he complain that he is never treated well? Is he jealous or trying to get revenge? Does she flaunt her sin? If this evidence is present in someone, Jesus is not. Even if they pray using his name, it means nothing. If the phone is dead, it doesn't matter if you dial the right number. If the phone line is dead, saying words into the mouthpiece doesn't change anything.

But when we abide in Jesus, our lives change. The false happiness promised by evil becomes real joy. When Jesus comes in, sin goes out. When we abide in him and he in us, we are able to do good things. We are able to be a part of something important. When we abide in him and he in us, life and goodness seem to become a part of our lives in ways we could not imagine. When Jesus in central to our lives, opportunities present themselves to us. Doors open. We get blessed in so many different ways we can't even count them all.

In verse seven, Jesus says, "If you abide in me, and my words abide in you, ask for whatever you wish and it shall be done for you." When Jesus' words abide in us, we are memorizing, reading and striving to keep them. We want to know more of what he said and did. The words of the Bible are life to those of us who believe. We want more of them in our hearts and our minds. When his words abide in us, the very things that we want change. People who are really bearing fruit get blessed over and over, sometimes in inexplicable ways. Miracles happen.

Do you want Jesus to abide even more in your life? Are you willing for him to replace sin in your life? Are you willing to let go of the sin in your life? Even if on your own you have not been able to remove it? Have you realized that we are powerless to do good without him? Are you inviting him in?

It is my prayer that every one of us can answer "yes" to every one of these questions. Amen.

Feeling Real Love
Jn 15:9-17

Many of us realize late that we rejected the wrong commands.

Hearing that God loves us is difficult for many of us to accept. We so want to be loved but we have been deeply disappointed by people who said they loved us but did not evidence real love. So it is hard to accept these words from Jesus. We want to. It's just that the word and the idea of love have gotten so distorted that it is hard for us to know what they mean, let alone accept them. Even if we trust Jesus and understand what his love means, many of us do not feel worthy of being loved. We struggle with shame over the sin we've committed. We remember it and are plagued by it through temptation and self-criticism. Yet being important to someone and to God is what we want. We want to feel cared about, valued and protected.

Evil tries to exploit our need and uses it to trick and trap us. God wants to give us love so we will be protected from evil. We will be able to withstand temptation because our basic need for love is being fulfilled. Jesus tells us he loves us like the Father has loved him. He gives to us what he received from God. The Bible teaches us that all love comes from God, that He is love. This is fact as surely as the sunlight comes from the sun. Yet, not everything that gets labeled love is love.

Jesus tells us how to receive love and what to do to keep it. He tells us to abide in his love and to do so, we must keep God's commandments. We are to love one another as he loved us. In Greek, real love is expressed by the word "agape." It means *to want the best for us, to desire that good things happen for us.* It means *to treat others the way we want to be treated.* Real love has no strings attached to it as in "I'll love you if . . ." Real love doesn't want control. It wants us to have control of our choices and ourselves. Real love does not want to exploit us. It wants only good for us. The great thing is that the more we experience God's love through others, the less vulnerable we become to being exploited. When we experience real love, we can tell the cheap imitations that would like to exploit us and use us.

When Jesus tells us we are to love one another, he is telling us that this is a sign that we are letting his love in. When we feel really important and cared about, we want to share that love with others. We want to pass onto others what we have received. Then, the more we give, the more capacity we have to receive even more love and pass on even more. It is like a fountain that is filled by a spring and then gives water to others.

Inside of this one command to love one another are the Ten Commandments. They are about love and respect. They spell out how we are to treat others, their property and God. It is part of the great paradox that to have freedom we must live with commands, rules and boundaries. Loving others, God and self means respecting God, others and self. That can only be done by loving with restrictions on our lives. Evil will try to tell us that God just wants to take away our freedom and keep us from the good stuff. Nothing could be farther from the truth.

Real love is freely caring and can only occur in the presence of truth, honesty and boundaries. In the absence of truth, human beings put on masks, take on roles, are phony, create illusions, and delude themselves. People living this way cannot be close to anyone because of their secrets. If they were close to someone, their lies might become known, revealed by their intentions, desires and actions. To the degree that we play roles, we have been deceived. To the degree that we sin, we have been deceived. To the degree that we don't like God's rules in our lives, we have been deceived.

When we live within God's boundaries and respect His commandments, we can learn to trust others and ourselves more. This is because the more honest we are, the more we can detect dishonesty in others. And conversely, the more dishonest we are, the more we see the honesty that exists in some others. The more dishonest we are, the more we see others who are for God. Part of the cost of being dishonest is that it distorts our ability to detect dishonesty.

Jesus tells us that he wants our joy to be full. He wants us to be safe, protected and able to receive blessings that are there for us. The most exciting and joyful life is one that lives by the constraints God gives us. This means that we stop gossiping even if we think it feels good to do it. This means that we are willing to live by the truth, even if it means we stop being manipulative or being manipulated. This means living by God's rules because they are there, whether or not we understand why we ought or ought not to follow them. Our compliance says we are willing to follow Jesus. It says that we have accepted his love and love him as well. We have seen what sin does to our life and we want to be able to respect ourselves. All we really need to do is confess, repent and ask. Confess our sin, be willing to repent of it by leaving it alone, and ask for His forgiveness.

It is my prayer that each of us is willing to receive the forgiveness that is ours to receive, so that we can go and love one another even more. Amen.

Real love casts out fear.

This passage is part of Jesus' prayer for his followers. Knowing that he was leaving them and that they needed his protection, Jesus prayed for them. Many of us have done the same thing when we have had to leave loved ones. We have asked God to keep them safe. It's how we deal with being away from our family and friends, and it's one of the ways we express our love. We do the most important thing we can: We pray.

Notice that Jesus prayed that his disciples be kept safe from the evil one. He prayed for their spiritual safety, knowing that evil would attack them. We would do well to pray in a similar way. By being concerned first with the kingdom of Heaven, we get our priorities straight. We need to do this. Then the rest will be taken care of. Many of us have been concerned first with our own and with others' physical, emotional and social safety and only then about our spiritual safety. We pray for everything under the sun sometimes, when we really need to pay attention to how Jesus teaches us to pray. If someone is spiritually protected from evil and sin, this covers everything that is important. Sin brings death, destruction, loss and separation. Being protected from evil gives us protection from the worst things. Isn't it better to be found than to be lost for eternity?

Sin brings the most difficulties to our lives. Sin separates us from God, each other and ourselves. It steals our ability to get close to others and to maintain the types of relationships we want with the ones we love. Evil uses sin to erect blocks to real love. Evil never wants real love because real love casts out fear. All sin is rooted in the soil of fear. Evil wants us to be fooled into pseudo-love or dependency. Most of us have lost much because evil stole love from us, either in our own lives or before we were born. It stole from our parents the ability to be close by leading them to live with sin. It may have plagued them with pride, envy, bitterness or loss. Evil attacked them with addictions, fear, superstitions and foolish ideas about God. For some of us, our ancestors were loving people, but they were too rigid or too accepting. We may have thought that it was our sin that was causing us problems but sin is often multi-generational.

Evil wants to steal our blessings, love, strength and health. It wants to take from us anything we have that is good. Evil tells us that by ignoring God's commandments, we can get the good things, that only fools and lesser people have to live by God's laws. Yet God tells us that by living with His commandments, we get the good things, like relationships built on integrity, love, loyalty and honor. All of these qualities come from God. Thinking that we can get them from evil or thinking that they will remain in God's absence is like thinking the light will stay after the sun has gone down.

Real joy, love, peace and happiness come from God. He tells us they are free gifts. He also tells us we must live by His Word, not by whatever emotion with which evil prompts us. From a spiritual perspective, all of this makes a lot of sense. Evil wants chaos, drama, hurt feelings, loss and destruction. This happens most easily when people do not live by God's Word, when they do not live with restraint and within guidelines. Love cannot be built on a foundation of dishonesty, secrets and lies. It cannot flourish in a place of sin. It cannot grow or live without truth. There is really only one source of truth and that is God. Evil will try to distort truth as a way to manipulate, lie, trick and deceive.

Jesus gave God's Word to his disciples and to us. We are not of the world. Our goals, our allegiance and our final destination are different from those of the world. And sometimes the world hates us because of this. As Jesus knew his disciples would be attacked, we may be attacked, too. Evil in the world will look for cracks in our spiritual armor. Sometimes this will happen through criticism. Sometimes it will happen through judgment, which evil will try to use to weaken and disillusion us. When God judges us, there is room for change, an opportunity to repent and be spared. God's forgiveness, love and Word are stronger. God's Word brings us health, forgiveness, happiness and peace. Jesus tells us that he did not come to condemn but to preserve. Abiding in God's Word brings us blessings that we could not even dream of. God's work heals hurts, binds up old wounds and gives us new sight and new life.

There are other ways evil tries to work. It tricks us into hating people, instead of hating the evil that is working in them. Sometimes evil tricks us by leaving us with hurt feelings. When evil steals our thankfulness, it steals some of our blessings. Evil can cause loving people to turn away from love. Our God is stronger but we have to use His principles, His Word and His perspectives. Otherwise, we are vulnerable, like sheep that become easy pickings when they stray from the flock. Faith is stronger. No matter what our situation, we can "Enter His gates with thanksgiving and into His courts with praise."

It is my prayer that we can see that God rewards us and wants to bless us, that He abides by what He has given, that He is truthful and that He upholds what He has already said. Amen.

21

Learning To Listen Is An Important Step
              Jn 16:5-15; Joel 2:28-32; Acts 2:1-13

Through Jesus' teaching, we can better understand the Holy Spirit.

In verses 5 and 6 of John 16, Jesus has just told the disciples that he is
leaving them and they become very, very sad. Their deep grief is familiar
to all of us. We have all grieved over loved ones who have passed. Some
of us have grief over present circumstances. Many of us have grief about
lost dreams and fallen hopes. So we can understand the disciples' grief.
We can also realize that the Holy Spirit comforted the disciples and be
similarly comforted. And we can be comforted by what Jesus said to his
followers. He encouraged them to know that it would be better for them if
he left. He told them the Holy Spirit couldn't come to them unless he left.
This idea doesn't really make sense while we are in the middle of grief. It's
when we reach the other side of grief that it begins to.

One of God's blessings is that He gives us the ability to have even deeper
relationships with others when we have had loving relationships in our
past. Even if our loved ones have died or left, by being part of a loving
relationship, we have learned how to relate to others in an intimate, deep
and meaningful way. Our family members and friends are irreplaceable.
No one can ever really take the place of a mother, father, brother, sister,
child, grandchild or beloved friend. And yet, in another sense, this is what
can happen for us. We can experience the people we have lost through
others. As humans, we tend to recreate and refine the relationships we
have had in the past. If we loved someone and were loved by them, we
can experience that same kind of relationship with others.

Of course, if we experienced negative relationships in our past, we may
tend to repeat those, too, until we learn how to be free of the pattern.
People who were abused when they were young often find someone to
abuse them in the present. Or, sometimes, a victim becomes an abuser.
This is not changing. Real change occurs when we neither abuse nor are
abused. Real change occurs when we change spiritually. This kind of
change impacts everything in our lives.

Perhaps we have needed to forgive in order to be free. Perhaps we've
needed to be forgiven and to forgive. Perhaps we've needed to develop
faith, to understand and then follow God's laws. Perhaps we've just
needed to believe. Whatever change we need to make, the Holy Spirit can
guide, lead and direct us.

Part of changing spiritually is realizing the role sin plays in our lives. Sin
makes us miss God's blessings. Sin separates us from God and His ways,
and thus blocks real love. Real love cannot be based on sin. Jesus told his

disciples that the Holy Spirit would reprove the world of sin. The revised standard version of the Bible translates the word "reprove" as *convince*. The Holy Spirit points out our sin to us just as it points out our real righteousness. Especially, the Holy Spirit shows us good and evil. Verses 8 and 9 of John 16 say, "And when he comes, he will prove the world wrong about sin and righteousness and judgment . . ." Not believing in Jesus is sin, in part because this disbelief infers that Jesus and the Bible are liars. It rejects Jesus and God. People who do not believe say that they can do it themselves. They can't. They need God. We all do.

The verses in John 16 continue, saying that the Holy Spirit will chastise the world regarding righteousness. The world's righteousness is false. It isn't God's righteousness. The praise, celebrity or glamour bestowed on someone depends on what's in fashion at the time. When we focus on these things, we are looking away from God's righteousness, and we are rejecting God. The world's righteousness ignores the spiritual battle and real spiritual growth. The world's righteousness embraces pride, it negates God's laws, and it leads to destruction, depression and death through the pursuit of harmful ways of living.

Jesus told his disciples that the Holy Spirit would also judge the world. It lets us know when evil is near. It lets us know what is evil and who is acting in an evil way toward us. It lets us distinguish between what is sin and what isn't. These judgments will always be in line with the Bible and will always lift up Jesus and his teachings. Sometimes, the world will try to deceive us and we'll think that something we are doing is fine when it is really about sin. Yet, the Holy Spirit will confront us. It is possible, however, to stop listening to the Holy Spirit and thus to stop being informed. People who do this lose their way. They cannot even tell when they lie to themselves. You are all right as long as the Holy Spirit is confronting you with your sin and you can hear it.

The most profound way we can experience the Holy Spirit is to acknowledge our sin when it is pointed out to us. The Holy Spirit guides us toward truth. You can feel it in your soul, as in the times you have been about to sin and something nudged at you, telling you it was wrong. The more we listen to this voice, the more blessed we become. How well we receive the Holy Spirit accounts for whether or not we grow spiritually.

It is my prayer that it becomes ever clearer to each of us how the Lord confronts, comforts and cleans us. Amen.

22

Being Born Anew
Jn 3:1-8, Isa 6:1-8, Rom 8:12-17

What we value most owns us.

This passage is about being born anew, about getting a second change at things. It's about realizing our mistakes, about learning to see sin clearly, and about wanting to repent. It's about learning to see the kingdom of Heaven.

By the world's standards, Nicodemus was a good man. Outwardly, he demonstrated the signs of faith. He held a position of authority in his city. But Nicodemus was deluding himself in regards to his own sin and his faith. He was probably one of those offensive people who seem oblivious to how much they hurt others or to how evil distorts their perceptions. Haven't we all known people like this? People whose sin and denial of sin has blocked their ability to self-assess? People who delude themselves about how much they hurt, anger and insult others? Through denial, they think and act as though they are fine inside and as though they are good to others. Their words and actions demonstrate otherwise, though. The stubborn denial of people like Nicodemus leaves us challenged to cope with them. People like Nicodemus are focused only on themselves.

Yet haven't we all been a little bit like Nicodemus? We've lost patience with others because of our own sin. We've been in denial about things we've done against others or ourselves. So we can't always rely on our own notion of whether or not we are close to God. At times, we too easily delude ourselves about our own sin. Fortunately, Nicodemus began coming to his senses. He went to see Jesus, but at night, his pride so great that he did not want to tarnish the esteem in which he imagined people held him. (No doubt many people were not fooled at all by Nicodemus' sin and denial of sin.) He said to Jesus, "Rabbi, we know that you are a teacher come from God, for no one can do these signs that you do, unless God is with them." At least Nicodemus was beginning to acknowledge Jesus' importance. But still, he began his sentence with " . . . we know. . . ." Nicodemus may not have known that his arrogance was showing.

We naturally dislike the arrogant, the pompous, the prideful and those in denial. These people can be hurtful. Sometimes, people like this know that others don't like them but they don't know why. Sometimes they don't even think about it. Yet haven't all of us been so wrapped up in ourselves and in our pain that we were oblivious to the pain of others? In our sinful pride and our refusal to see ourselves as others see us, there is some of Nicodemus in all of us. It can be tough when we first realize this about ourselves.

Jesus told Nicodemus, "Very truly, I tell you, no one can see the kingdom of God without being born from above." People who are like Nicodemus are in such pain that they cannot face the truth. Pride and arrogance create a shield so stout, they can keep from themselves evidence of the pain, sin and ugliness of their lives. To change, they must undergo a fundamental change, a new start as radical as a new birth. So that they can learn new things, they must be humble, as devoid of pride as a newborn baby.

Being born anew means being willing for God to come into our lives and to point out to us our sin—the dirt—and to help us clean it out. Being born anew means beginning with a clean slate. To reach this point, we must acknowledge our sin and our denial of it. We can only get to a new beginning when we allow ourselves to depend on God and on others.

It's easy to turn away from seeing our flaws, and yet, when we realize that we are children of God and are loved, we're more able to let go of our foolish pride. We can get there when we realize we are loved. This gives us the strength to assess ourselves honestly. Think about how newborn babies are so open to love and to learning. Just thinking about them and their innocence brings a smile to our faces. Thinking about older people who have been born anew can bring smiles to our faces, too. Poor Nicodemus was looking only at the world's view of things. He missed what Jesus was telling him about a new spiritual birth.

To Nicodemus, Jesus said, "Very truly, I tell you, no one can enter the kingdom of God without being born of water and Spirit. What is born of the flesh is flesh, and what is born of the Spirit is spirit." When we are born of the Spirit, we know we are loved. We can easily acknowledge our sin because we know that bringing sin to light helps us to overcome it. We can praise God for helping us to see this. When we are born of the Spirit, we know we are loved. Our intense thirst and hunger for righteousness leads us to see what we did no matter what it takes to see it. We know that admitting our sin frees us of it. Our love of God, His Word and His standards tell us we are heading in the right direction. When we are really born of the Spirit, we know we get blessed by confessing our sin. We know that Jesus wants us to have a new beginning—another chance—no matter what we have done or how many chances we have had in the past. It's a good exchange: We turn in sin, shame, filth, false pride, and arrogance. We get real self-esteem, a knowing that we are someone special. We are born anew.

It is my prayer that each of us can acknowledge the sin in our lives and know that acknowledging it is the only real path to peace through closeness to God. Amen.

If you have faith, you are in good company.

Jesus had been making a name for himself. When he went home, many crowded around to see him. People there had mixed feelings about him. Some were happy that a local was becoming famous and that he had come back home. There will always be some who will know and appreciate your success, especially your success in the Lord. People who are sincere about their faith will sense your faith. They will be happy for and about you. Other people, though, when they sense your faith in God, will not be happy. Some of Jesus' friends and family had heard rumors about him and wondered what was going on with this person they knew. Some thought he was crazy. It's ok when people think we're a little crazy after we've done bad things. But it's another matter when people think we're crazy because we have faith.

Sometimes, people say that very sincere Christians are crazy. It is one of the highest compliments we can receive that some people think we're crazy because we have honest faith. Perhaps you, too, have heard people called crazy who testify from their faith, or who tithe, or who give up criminal ways, or who refuse to do dope or be around those who do. When we are called crazy because we have profound faith, we are in very good company: Jesus, Paul, Francis of Assisi, C.S. Lewis, Mother Theresa, Mary Magdalene and others. God rewards and blesses our desire to serve Him. Desire to serve the Lord comes from appreciating the fact that you have been forgiven, cleansed and set free.

Jesus asks here, "How can Satan cast out Satan?" People accused Jesus of being evil, even though they saw him do good things. He asked them a question that contains a foundational truth in it. Evil cannot cast out evil. Our Christian tradition says that we cannot be good on our own. We do not have the ability to cast our evil—the dirt of our lives, if you will—on our own. The extent of our righteousness is like dirty clothes that need cleansing. We need God to be cleansed. People who try to begin a new good habit or to stop an old one know only too well how futile this can be without God's help.

All of us who have been changed by God know that the changes inside of us have come from God, not from our own willpower. We are grateful, not proud. We want to boast not about ourselves but about what God has done. We know it is God who cast out an addiction, hatred, shame, or our urge to do wrong. We can celebrate His deliverance of us.

Some of the people were saying that Jesus had an unclean spirit. They were mixed up, calling evil good and good evil. This is what can happen to us when we get very involved in sin. Evil can trick us so that we mix up good and evil. It can cause us to declare good what we know is wrong.

Here, Jesus tells us that blasphemy against the Holy Spirit is unforgivable. Calling Jesus evil is forgivable. Openly calling the Holy Spirit evil is not forgivable. We should be hesitant when we want to call evil someone who claims to be operating from faith. An unwillingness to recognize goodness and the actions of the good means the person cannot be forgiven because they refuse to recognize the One who forgives. It's like waiting for a cheque in the mail but you don't believe in the mailman. How are you going to get the cheque? If you don't believe in the Holy Spirit, how are you going to be forgiven? And without forgiveness, we are condemned to live with the pain of our sin: with shame, fear and anger, and without peace.

Declaring Jesus' teachings, preaching and actions as evil is blasphemy, meaning to speak reproachfully of, to rail at, to enjoy humiliating. We have no authority to belittle others' faith nor do we have any authorization to accuse without proof. When people belittle God's actions, they are in danger of the criticism backfiring on them. It is a basic truth of life that when we put down someone's belief in God that same standard ultimately hurts us.

We can take comfort, though, in knowing that the actions of the Holy Spirit to heal, encourage and help us will be defended. When people attack us as they did Jesus when they attacked the good that he did and the goodness in him that was from God, we will be protected. The evil done to us will be avenged, but not by us. It is comforting to realize that vengeance is God's work. If we have been one of those people who called evil good and good evil, let us pray to be forgiven. If we went so far as to refuse to hear God's correction, let us pray to be healed of the evil that caused that type of pride and stubbornness. If we have been guilty of blaspheming the Holy Spirit, then we have all the more reason to ask the Holy Spirit to come into our hearts and minds now, so that we will do better in the future. When we really love the Lord, one sin is too many. We want to be as clean as possible because we appreciate what He has done for us.

It is my prayer that if any of us have felt guilty of the unforgivable sin, we now know it meant we didn't want any connection with God. If there's a part of us that still enjoys, appreciates and desires closeness to God, even if we don't feel worthy, then God is still calling us. God is still calling you to a deeper relationship and to service. Amen.

Your Faith Can Grow
Mk 4: 26-34, Ezek 17:22-24, 2 Cor 5: 6-10

Even a little is enough.

Jesus taught us in parables because they teach us more than we could learn in other ways. We remember stories and parables because of their imagery and because they teach us on many levels. Jesus taught us in parables because they are a way of teaching us about faith that respects us and speaks to us about our journey, whether we are beginners or old hands at faith living. Parables can communicate a great deal in just a few words.

Most of us remember the story Jesus taught us about the mustard seed. One of the messages in the parable of the seed is about the Kingdom of God. We can notice in this story how it speaks about our faith, the Kingdom of God in our hearts and minds. If the seed is understood as the Word of God and the ground is our faith, we can recognize that God is telling us that through our faith, the Word of God grows. It changes our faith and produces a valuable harvest. Our faith produces the blade, then the ear, and finally the full grain on the ear. Our faith grows and evolves. It changes as we let the Word of God into our hearts and minds.

There are three stages to the development of faith: the beginning, the middle and maturity. When we first begin to delve into matters of faith, our faith is fragile and tentative. Like a blade of grain first breaking through the soil to light, it needs nurturing and protection. Hebrews tell us that faith comes from listening and hearing the Word of God. We can read the Bible, listen to a sermon, or remember things we hold in our minds.

For most of us, emotion drives our initial desire for faith. And at this stage, the danger to our faith comes from other emotions. When our faith evolves, we're less driven by the emotions that propel us to seek forgiveness and to be cleansed. Then, we must put forth conscious effort to reach out for God's Word. At this middle stage, people are sometimes tricked. They get fooled into thinking they have what they can get and what they need, when they really have a sustaining need for forgiveness. Making this transition requires perseverance. It requires sustained loyalty to receiving the Word of God regularly.

The third stage is where we begin to put our faith to work. At this stage, our faith is producing grain. James says, "Show me your faith and I'll show you my works," that without work our faith is dead. Ultimately, we put our faith into action, following God's Word for our own lives and by helping others. Faith that reaches maturity becomes the greatest of things that can grow. It can give us comfort. It can be how we receive guidance, help, health and happiness.

There is much work for us here. People are hurting from the past. We can bring comforting words and kindness to them. People are afraid because their health or the health of someone they love is compromised or declining. They need reassurance. Many people would appreciate you praying with them. There are people struggling with temptations. They need our prayers and our encouragement.

There are people who need the reassurance of people who have a loyalty to the truth. There are people who need positive role models and friends who will talk to them about faith, about the Bible and about their fears. There are people struggling to understand the Bible. They need our prayers, our encouragement and perhaps our guidance and knowledge. We can help protect the new believers, inspire the immature ones and encourage the old believers.

God needs and is calling each one of us. He has work for all of us. I don't know what God is calling you to do. That isn't for me to know. But I do know that you are being called. Whatever you are being called to do, God will richly bless you for doing it. Someone once said," If you see something that needs to be done, then you are the one being called to do it."

Whatever we put into our minds will grow. If we put God's Word into our minds, we get faith. If we put in arguments, worldly loyalty to non-believers or the trash of the world, it will grow into weeds of sin, discontent, irritability and disbelief. This can happen so gradually that we seldom notice it until we see the effects. What we dwell on has an effect on our hearts and minds, and on our behavior. What we think about and gather around us builds either faith and health or disbelief and despair. A mustard seed is small. Often, we belittle our faith because it is small and we think it can't do much. An atom is small. Yet a split atom is an atomic bomb. Size has nothing to do with power. God's power is in that mustard seed. God's power is enough if it were half the size of a mustard seed because it is God's power. God has given each of us a measure of faith. No matter its size, we can encourage and nurture it with prayer and with God's Word.

It is my prayer that each of us recognize a little more of how important we are to God, and that we become even more willing to put our faith to work. I also pray that we are able to demonstrate how we are allowing our faith to change us from the inside out. Amen.

There is still someone with whom we can be astonished every day.

Jesus was teaching on the Sabbath in the community where he grew up and many people were astonished. They did not have faith in him, so they were astonished at his teaching. Instead of realizing who Jesus was and that all real truth comes from God, the people were questioning, "Where did this man get all this?" They were committed to their pride, not to being receptive to God. They were more afraid to receive a blessing from someone they knew than from a stranger. This is often true. Our families and others familiar with us may be the last to recognize some of our major changes. They treat us like we are younger and unknowing, or like our commitment to God is temporary. It's as though they keep seeing us as we were.

Have you noticed how some people criticize others to boost themselves up? Alcoholics and drug addicts are especially bad about finding blame and criticizing others. The missing ingredient for them is God. Without a spiritual change, a person hasn't really changed. They may show willpower, but it is only with the power of God in our lives that something much more dramatic can happen. Our God is an awesome God who brings good things to us. The people of Nazareth blocked God's blessings. Their lack of faith kept them from receiving the type of miracles that others received. Sometimes, this is how the world views faith. People who reject the world's view in favor of God's are criticized or rejected.

Romans 10:17 says, "Faith comes by hearing and hearing the Word of God." I don't know if this means that we must hear the Word of God over and over, or if it means that faith produces hearing and hearing produces faith. Either way, we're required to hear the Word of God. What a blessing it is to know that the Word of God is living and active. It changes us from the inside out. Sometimes, I can tell when people are reading their Bibles and when they have stopped. There is a special peace that comes to someone who is drawing closer to God.

For all of us, it becomes a choice. Are we going to look for the ways in which God speaks to us? Or will we choose not to? We can hear God's Word through Scripture. We can hear it through song. Sometimes God speaks to us through people we know, sometimes through people we don't know. We are not told to believe everything that others say. . . . and yet, when we decide to listen for God's direction, it sometimes comes from unlikely places.

Jesus' response to the people's lack of faith and to their criticism of him was to teach an eternal truth. A prophet is not without honor except in his own country and among his own kin. People that know us are often surprised we demonstrate the power of God to change us. They are skeptical and judge us by their own limitations. The people of Nazareth had watched Jesus grow up. They knew him. They did not think that the young man they had known ought to be able to perform miracles anymore than they could. They could not perform them, so why should Jesus be able to?

But how often we are sent to the people that can bless us. When God sends us on missions, it's not just for the other person. There is almost always a lesson for us to learn as well. When our faith is open to God speaking to us, it doesn't matter if the person speaking is male or female, young or old, or any color of the rainbow. The group we don't think could teach us anything is the group that often teaches us the most. Our God wants to do miraculous things in our lives. Often, it is our lack of faith that blocks those miracles. It is our lack of faith that keeps us from even seeing the opportunities. Many more lives can be changed by God's miraculous power. There are people who need to be free of addictions and self-destructive compulsions, free from an act or a life of crime, free from a negative view of themselves, free to love and serve the Lord, and free to receive the blessings He has for us.

I encourage you to pray for a revival of faith so that His power and His grace can be seen more powerfully. Does it take mountainous faith? Jesus told us of faith the size of a mustard seed. If we have faith, it is God's power operating, not ours. When we know that God's power is not limited by our power, that it is bigger than us, we can get blessed. We can be looking for His blessings, expecting His miracles, listening for His voice. He may be calling you now to begin healing or to surrender to His will for your life. I know that He wants to bless us. He wants to bless you. Will you let Him bring you peace? Will you let Him lead you to green pastures, beside still waters, and to the people He sends you to, so that both of you can be blessed?

It is my prayer that each of us expands the ways in which we are willing for God to reach us. I pray that our hearts become so excited from hearing God's Word that we can encourage those who have not yet met the One who can set us free. Amen.

26

Finding Freedom
Mk 6:7-13, Am 7:12-17, Eph 1: 3-10

On whom do you depend? It makes all the difference in this world—and in the next.

Mark says, "And he called to him the twelve and began to send them out two by two and give them authority over the unclean spirits." We might ask why Jesus sent the disciples out two by two. Perhaps there is a clue in Scripture and in our own lives. Built inside of us is the desire for closeness to other people. Sometimes we notice a lack of closeness by a deep inner sense of loneliness. At other times it manifests itself through a self-destructive behavior we use to try to overcome our need.

The way the Bible puts it is that God saw that it was not good for people to be alone. People can more easily take advantage us when we feel lonely. During these times, we're apt to make poor decisions about friends, lovers, our lifestyles and our futures. We'll ignore warning signs about a person's character and our own awareness that there is danger nearby. When depressed with loneliness, we seldom make good decisions. We're so desperate to have a friend or a success.

In sending the disciples out two by two, Jesus ensured that each would have a like-minded faith friend. The disciples would be less likely to act out of their desire to be liked by those with whom they spoke. They would be less likely to feel a need to belong to another group. They would be safer. Isn't this also true for us? When we spend time with a friend with whom we feel safe, we are more likely to act in our own best interest.

Jesus told his disciples to take nothing with them on their journeys except a staff. . . . no bread, money or bag. They were to carry no extra clothing and to wear sandals. Sandals meant someone was a free person, not a slave. Jesus was saying that the disciples were free. They took no food and would be dependent on others for their meals and their lodging. Being totally dependent helps us learn to trust and to see in different ways the goodness of God, sometimes acting through other people. The disciples would carry nothing in which to put money. They were to accept only food and lodging. This is all pretty radical, isn't it? A sort of boot camp experience in sandals. Can you imagine beginning a journey so barely provisioned?

Each disciple carried a staff, a simple item used as a walking stick. People of faith think of Moses and other prophets using a staff. It was a symbol of their humility and their dependence on God. We would do well to carry a symbol of our faith, too. Christians recognize a fish or a rooster as a symbol of their faith. To the world, these symbols might seem foolish, nothing that connotes courage, strength, beauty or commitment. And yet they do, because they refer to God's strength.

Today, for day-to-day living, this lifestyle would not be practical but it can be a model for our spiritual discipline. We learn to rely on God more heavily when we don't have other backup. When the Hebrew people were in the wilderness, they were dependent on God. God gave them manna and told them to get enough food to last just one day at a time, except on the day before the Sabbath, the only time the extra food would not go bad. Isn't it true for most of us in looking back over difficult times, we see that God did provide for us? It may not have been what we asked for, and yet, over the long haul, it was something that was even more helpful to us.

It seems that sin blocks our ability to depend on God. Sin separates us from and steals our trust in God, others and ourselves. The disciples set out preaching that people should repent. This remains a primary focus of Christianity. Repentance is our faith's cornerstone. Jesus began his ministry with the words, "Repent and believe." He encouraged his followers to practice personal repentance and to encourage others to do the same. You may find yourself thinking about what you need to do to repent. Perhaps there are long ago sins or recent ones. Perhaps you're just thinking about something sinful. Repentance is an attitude that is required for us to be Christians. It means we wish we could redo our sin. It is soul-deep realization that our sin was wrong and we regret committing it or thinking about it.

During this time, evil may try to trick us into not accepting forgiveness. But the very fact that we remain sorry and want to change our lives means that we are capable of repentance. Repentance implies that we have accepted God into our lives in a powerful way. Forgiveness frees us from the past. We can continue to repent and to encourage others. As God's representatives, we're obliged to tell others about their need for repentance, much as the disciples did. We can do this by example or by talking with them about their sin in a supportive way. Like the disciples, we have authority over unclean spirits.

It is my prayer that each of us becomes such an example to others. I also pray that we experience and feel deeply the forgiveness that God has for us each time we repent. This is how His grace works best, to encourage others to find the freedom of the Lord. Amen.

27

Faith Makes Things Happen
                 Jn 6:1-15, 2 Kings 4:42-44, Eph 4: 1-6, 11-16

The most important things cannot be taken from us.

A multitude followed Jesus because they saw or heard about the miracles where he was healing the sick. People came with many motivations. Some were eager because of the excitement, in today's vernacular, the "buzz." They were looking for adventure and entertainment. Later they would get an additional rush from telling others about seeing the miracle-worker. Some people were interested because they needed or wanted a miracle cure for themselves or for loved ones. Some people had seen or heard about Jesus' miracles and believed him to be the Christ. They felt that he was truly close to God, and they just wanted to hear his wisdom and be close to him. They were seeking closeness to God and to a godly person.

If we are really following Jesus, there will be changes in our lives. The thrill seekers and those following out of habit or some other ulterior motive are unlikely to change, unless they are seeking closeness to God. When we really follow Jesus, we change. When he touches our lives, we are different. We begin to want to avoid sin. In fact, we begin to hate sin for what it has done to us and to others. Having a real and personal relationship with Christ has a profound effect on our lives and on our view of the world. We begin to want to be free of sin because we begin to know what it feels like to be good and clean. We want more of this feeling.

There is a clear truth: When someone has no real change of heart and mind, Jesus in not in his or her life. Attending services just to go to them or be seen there doesn't show a real change. It doesn't matter how elegantly a churchgoer sings or prays. It doesn't matter how many verses of the Bible they can quote. It doesn't matter how often they attend church. If there is no real change and the sin continues, they do not know Jesus. Jesus said we would know people by their fruit. If self-proclaimed Christians commit blatant, unrepented sins and are making no effort to change, they do not know Jesus. If there is an abundance of the fruits of the flesh, they do not know Jesus. If there is much sin, bitterness, greed, envy, jealousy and open disregard for God's laws, there's no argument. There is no Jesus in their lives. When people really want Jesus in their lives, they follow what he says and they change. What they cannot do, they struggle with until he gives them victory over sin. When this happens to you, you begin to show in your actions that the Lord Jesus Christ has touched you. When you have felt overwhelmed by his love, when you have found this peace and know that you have not been left out, you have joy, happiness and contentment. You don't want to trade it for one moment of sin and a lifetime of guilt.

Jesus went to Philip directly and questioned him. He tested Philip with a question in order to teach him. It wasn't a question to see if he would sin. God doesn't tempt us. God provides us with opportunities to learn from our experiences. Jesus provided Philip with an opportunity to see how far his learning had taken him. Jesus speaks directly to us and he is always urging us to learn. He is inviting us to a closer, more important and more satisfying relationship with him. To have these things, we often must come out of our old ways of seeing the world and ourselves. Throughout his ministry, Jesus was teaching by example, by questioning, by telling stories and by using parables. These all were designed to wake us up, to change our perspectives and to alter our experiences.

Jesus asked Philip, "Where are we to buy bread so these people may eat?" It seemed a simple question; yet understanding its implications meant that Philip would more deeply understand that our faith and dependence on God are what makes things happen. Philip told Jesus that six month's worth of wages would not feed all the people. Our efforts to change without Jesus are about as futile. It is when we really trust in Jesus that the miraculous happens. Miracles happen through faith. Our faith, our dependence on God, provides the arena where God performs His miracles.

You may have seen people who are these living, breathing miracles. You notice them because of the changes they made in their lives. They are different. You can hear the change in how they talk. You notice the change in their spirit manifested by their sense of calm. If you are one of these people who really know Jesus and are a living example of how he changes people, let's praise God. A miracle has happened in your life. If you are someone who has little or no change in your life, it's time to ask God into your life, truly to take Him into your heart to allow Him to change you from the inside out.

Is it time to repent, to get on your spiritual knees, and to pray for Him to really come into your life? If He does, then the sin will go. We can't have both a commitment to God and a commitment to sin. It is a clear truth.

It is my prayer that each of us begins to realize that Jesus can take care of us and perform miracles in us. I pray that we come to know that he can truly teach us, and lead us into deeper and deeper awareness of his love and his ways of seeing, so we will be blessed even now and in the future. Amen.

Being alone is vastly different from being lonely.

We see in this passage that the apostles returned to Jesus and told him all that they had taught and done. It's still good for us today to tell Jesus what we have said and done. Prayer is certainly one way to do this. Now, God does not need for us to tell him what we have done. Prayer is for us! As we pray, we can feel a quickening in our own spirit, letting us know if what we did was in line with God or not. With prayer, you can review your day with someone who really cares about you, who really wants to know, and who will comment if you are willing to listen. Real prayer means being committed in our relationship with God. It means being committed to knowing that He can and will lead us to good paths. It means that you trust in Him and want to have a deep, satisfying relationship with Him.

We can spend time praying for our loved ones and other people we know. Many of us do. We can let God know about our struggles with the difficult people whom we encounter, especially praying for the people who treat us badly. We can express to God our feelings of shame, fear, anger, sadness and guilt. God created us to feel. He can hear all about all of our emotions and love us still. In fact, when you express your deepest feelings and your struggles to God, you can notice how your feelings begin to change. You'll notice that how through your faith, you begin to feel healthier. When we go to God in prayer, we are checking in with Him the way the disciples did.

Jesus said to his disciples, "Come away to a deserted place all by yourselves and rest awhile." He had heard their reports and then he gave them a prescription, of sorts. A quiet place can be a place of rest and sanctuary. How often have we resisted being in that quiet place, fearing our feelings of loneliness? Instead, we can welcome this place as one where we can encounter God more intimately. Jesus, Paul, Mary, David, Elizabeth (John's mother)—all people of faith—ultimately spent time alone with God. Often, when we're caught in the business of our family and social lives, we can't see new options. We don't let the Lord speak to us and guide us. Our time of rest must be more than a 30-second prayer or two minutes of reading Scripture. We can pray, think, meditate, walk, reflect, and empty our minds of distractions, and know that real rest comes from God.

As the disciples traveled and taught, there were many people they encountered who wanted a lot from them. Yet Jesus told them to go to a quiet place, be alone, and rest. This means that they had to say "no" to some things. Part of our spiritual training is knowing when and how to take rests. It means sometimes saying "no," regardless of the emotions others report to us. We can say "no" because we know we are doing what God expects of us. When someone is dependent on us, his or her needs can eat into our time alone with God. And it's easy for us to be seduced into thinking that we are that important. It's all right to set limits sometimes.

The world and God disagree profoundly on some things, especially regarding feelings. The world tells us that our feelings should direct our actions. The Bible is clear, however, that following our feelings around all of the time is like a dog following its tail. Our emotions follow from what we do and what we tell ourselves. If we want to change our emotions then, after prayer, we need to do something different so that our emotions have something new from which to develop. Our emotions are indicators. They give us information. They are not our leader.

Verse 34 says, "As Jesus landed he saw a great crowd and he had compassion on them because they were like sheep without a shepherd; and he began to teach them many things." If we are truly helping someone, we understand that this is God working through us. We are humble.

The people in this passage came wanting healing and other things from the disciples. How like them we are. We want God to speak to us personally and to do for us, to change things for us. We may have been hurt, disappointed and angry because God didn't or hasn't given us what we want. But isn't it a little arrogant for us to ignore the teachings He has already provided for us? From Isaiah 40: 31, we hear, " . . . those who wait for the Lord shall renew their strength, they shall mount up with wings like eagles, they shall run and not be weary, they shall walk and not faint." When we let God be our source of energy and motivation, it's easy to feel renewed. When we wait for the Lord, it's easy to start again, to recommit to our faith, to do more, to become new people.

God has called all of us, but only those who show our love for Him are chosen. We can show this love by following His commandments. Even when we fall short, we are not freed from the obligation of trying to keep them. Perhaps God is calling you to repent or to repent and rest. Perhaps He is calling you to go forth and tell others about Jesus. It may be that you are called to show God's power through the changes you've made in your own life.

It is my prayer that each of us recognizes that we are called by God, and that we not only listen to the Word but act upon it as well. Amen.

God Is Close By
Jn 6: 24-35, Ex 16: 2-4. 12-15, Eph 4:17-24

If you stop looking so hard for a sign, you may see one.

The passage begins with, "So when the crowd saw that neither Jesus nor his disciples were there, they themselves got into boats and went to Capernaum, looking for Jesus." The people were determined to find Jesus. Determination of this kind is successful. When people make up their minds that they are going to get closer to God, they can.

Just like those ancient peoples, people today go to elaborate lengths to find God. They put themselves through tests and long journeys. Some people have struggled through difficult times and long hours. Some have struggled through humiliation and even degradation to be close to God. Others have performed selfless acts of giving, healing and helping others in need. Still others have sought God through study and prayer. Yet we come to our searches with different motives. Some of us have pure hearts as we seek God. Others may have ulterior motives; they want something or they want God to do something for them. We see this in church, where as many as two-thirds of the people may be attending for less than spiritual reasons. Each of us can look into ourselves at our motives for seeking God and see if we are pure in our intentions.

That day long ago, when the people caught up with Jesus, he confronted them. He said, "Very truly, I tell you, you are looking for me not because you saw signs, but because you ate your fill of the loaves. Do not work for the food that perishes, but for the food that endures for eternal life, which the Son of Man will give you."

Sometimes, when we examine our motivations for not following Jesus, we find that we have fears of giving up a security blanket comprising a chase for money, sex, dishonest living or other similar pursuits. We have been putting these things ahead of God in our lives. We might also have purer reasons mixed in: We want to feel accepted and appreciated. We want to know that we matter. We can go to God for these things.

That day the people asked, "What must we do to perform the works of God? " They knew that their motives were mixed and needed improvement. Jesus replied, "This is the work of God, that you believe in him whom he has sent." We are still to believe in him whom God sent. This is what sets us apart as Christians, that we believe in Jesus as the Messiah, as the one who can show us the way to God's love and truth. This does not mean that we are superior to other religions. It means that we see Jesus as showing us the way to divine love and truth. For this, we owe Jesus our thanks, loyalty and appreciation. We pray in Jesus' name because this is what he taught us to do. We believe in him not because of some sign, but because he came into our hearts and changed our lives.

Jesus told us not to labor for food that perishes, but for food that endures to eternal life. When we're honest with ourselves, a lot of us spend our time on worthless pursuits. All of us have been tricked by the world into valuing things that have no lasting value. "If I just get that, I'll feel worthwhile," we tell ourselves. The world can deceive us, promising us importance, popularity and self-esteem when we pursue certain material goods or activities. But really, these things fade. They go in and out of fashion. People around us change. They may work against us. It's when we come to Jesus wanting first and foremost to do his will that we get real substance, value and self-esteem. Some of us have this peace. Others of us are looking for it. Jesus said, "Seek first the kingdom of Heaven and all the rest shall be added onto you."

That day, when he told the people to believe, some of them wanted a sign. Proof. In the early stages of faith, many people look for signs, even though they already know what sin is and what it isn't. As we mature in our faith, we see signs of verification of our faith in many places. We can sense God leading us to righteousness. We can see blessings. We know when He has made us to lie down in green pastures and has led us beside still waters. We know when Scripture, a sermon, a song or a friend's conversion and rebirth have comforted us. We sense the presence of goodness and faith in some people, and we sense its absence in others. As we mature in our faith, we see signs everyday. And because of our faith, even when we have sinned, we can repent, ask for forgiveness and get a clean slate. We get a new heart. This is part of Christianity's grace.

Each of us knows some of what God is calling us to do today. We may be called to believe. We may be called to repent so that we can believe. He may want us to surrender our wills and our contaminated hearts and minds, so that we may be cleansed. We may be called to live by different motives, interests and values. We may be called to live with a clean heart and a right mind, and to thank God for what He has done and continues to do in our lives. We may know that we are forgiven, and we know that we don't thank God enough for this. You may be called to believe that He wants you to have good things and be cared about. You may be called to recognize that He wants to bless you more. You may be called to notice the ways He is blessing you right now.

It is my prayer that each of us more fully know the love He has for us, and that we become more willing to renounce sin in favor of receiving even more of His blessings. Amen.

There is a big difference between wisdom and knowledge.

This invitation to wisdom is poetic. We're invited to a feast prepared for us at a House of Seven Pillars, which is a sacred place, a place of God. I'm reminded of the Shaker hymn " 'Tis a gift to be simple." Those who are simple are invited to the house of wisdom. And it's only the simple who are invited—only those of us who recognize how unable we are to get there on our own. This state of being simple isn't an insult to us. It's acknowledging how naïve we have been. All of us have been deceived. All of us have made mistakes. We trusted when we shouldn't have because evil took advantage of us.

Wisdom in this passage is portrayed as a woman inviting us to receive the blessings that are offered to us. It's like a wise old grandmother, who has prepared a feast for us if we will accept it. In Jewish law, women have a special relationship to wisdom. Women and mothers teach us about God. There may have been a mother or a grandmother and other women who treated you with kindness and showed you concern. It's also true that we teach others. We are always teaching others what we think about morality, what we think about God and how we think others ought to be treated. You have much wisdom from your faith and your experiences. You can draw on that wisdom and truth. It takes courage to follow this path, and to go against urges and temptations. But real wisdom knows which way lies sin and which is the way to truth and peace.

We all have the ability to eat at wisdom's banquet. Here, we can get the answers we need for any of life's questions. Many of them we already know. Yet our knowledge is incomplete until we can put it into practice and do what it is expected. Often, when people approach the Bible or prayer, they really don't know how to receive. They often say they don't know how to understand the Bible or how to pray. We need simply to be humble and open enough to receive, to know that we need God's wisdom to receive God's blessings. This is one of the gifts of simplicity.

The story is told about a student who seldom asked questions of others, who did not consult the books of wisdom, and who jumped to conclusions and quick answers. One day a teacher was filling the student's teacup and kept pouring even when the cup was full. The student cried, "Stop! The cup is full!" The teacher said, 'Yes, until the cup is full, no more will go in." Once we have chosen God's path, the answers—the wisdom—will come to us. When we come to the Scriptures in a simple—a humble—way, we let God and His word interpret for us. When we let go of our preconceived notions of what we will find, and instead become open to receive what God will tell us, we discover that His way is easier. It helps us and is better for us.

Wisdom says to us, "Come eat of my bread and drink of the wine I have mixed." God's wisdom wants us to be satisfied and content. Real everyday happiness and peace come from our relationship with God and from His wisdom. Yet we must put into practice the things that God requires of us. In Micah 6:8 we are told, "What does the Lord require of you but to do justice and to love kindness and to walk humbly with your God?" When we walk humbly with God, we receive many blessings. Our God wants to bless us. Just as you want to do for the people you love, so God wants to do for you.

Sin causes us to lose peace, patience and the companionship and love of good people in our lives. Sin never tells us that it is going to do this. Who would be so foolish as to follow sin if they knew it was deceiving them, and really bringing pain and sickness their way? Sin blocks us from receiving God's blessings. Sin separates us from ourselves, from each other and from God. It distorts our ability to think, act and be right. Walking humbly with God restores us to our right mind. Most of us know only too well what we need to eliminate from our lives. And we know the sin that is blocking us, whether it springs from loneliness or bitterness and whether it is fueled by hurt, fear or jealousy. We know only too well how sin robs us of life and love.

But what do we do next? How do we move forward to accomplish this change? The answer is that we can ask God to help us put these things aside. We can seek His path and His guidance so that we can feel better about ourselves. This is what is required: only that we be humble enough to ask for help and that we treat others with justice. We can do this because we know how we want to be treated and because we know what God expects of us. Walking humbly with God means allowing His wisdom to guide us, and choosing not to rely on our rationalizations. Wisdom has a feast prepared. Much planning and preparation has been done just for you! Many people talk about how God has a plan for you. This plan includes blessing you and leading you into paths of righteousness. It includes making you lie down in green pastures where there will be plenty for you. It includes leading you to still waters so you can be refreshed and so that you can live.

It is my prayer that we will all turn more to God and hear His invitation to eat at the feast which He has prepared for us. Amen.

Making Good Choices
Josh 24: 14-18, Jn 6: 60-69, Eph 5: 21-33

What we dwell on dwells in us.

God promises us a new beginning, one that leaves our sin behind. This is
our choice to make: We can remain with sin or we can hear how we are
called to choose our new beginning. In the time prior to where this verse
starts, people had not been living the way they should have been. Some
were worshipping other gods. Some were worshipping God by doing only
what was popular. Some were letting their fears rule them instead of their
faith. Through Joshua, God confronts the people and reminds them of
what He has done for them. You remember that God had delivered the
Hebrew people from slavery in Egypt. You may remember the mighty acts
of God that had taken place, such as God's delivery of manna in the
wilderness. As you read this, perhaps you will remember the ways that
God has delivered you. Perhaps you remember how much you wanted
God to be in your life, or how much God has brought you to a place of
change in your life.

The passage says, "Now therefore fear the Lord, and serve Him in sincerity
and faithfulness." There is so much wisdom in those words. When we fear
the Lord, we place Him first. When we are more afraid of losing God's
blessing than of losing a friend's acceptance, we are in a position to receive
a clean slate. We are putting God first, with all that that implies. Perhaps the
word *fear* would be better translated as "to have faith in or reverence of."
Yet the word does tell us something we really understand. So often we
human beings are driven by fear, whether it is a fear of not being or having
enough, a fear of loneliness, or a fear of embarrassment. These fears
ultimately cause us to sin. When we fear the Lord the most, we are able to
see God's blessings and to move away from sin.

Joshua told the people that day that if they were unwilling to serve God,
then they were to choose what god they would serve. Our lives, too, are
filled with choices. We choose whether we will serve the Lord or not.
Though we cannot choose all that happens to us, we can choose how we
respond to things. Our choices are what define us. They tell us what kind
of person we are and will be.

Every day, by the way we think about things and by the way we act, we
demonstrate if we have chosen to serve the Lord or not. We choose how
we treat others. We choose the language we use. If you sincerely seek to
do more of what God expects of you, then you will be blessed. As an old
song says, take one step and He will take two. If you are seeking to be
faithful to God, then you are already blessed. You can feel close to God,

and you already know the peace and quiet joy of a relationship that is beyond any other in the world.

If you haven't felt close to God, perhaps evil has been attacking you by throwing temptations and frustrations at you. Our lack of closeness to God can also occur because of our own lack of sincerity and faithfulness. Sometimes, we have a half-hearted desire to be close to God; what we really desire is something else. God wants our total commitment, though. And there is no way of fooling God. God knows your heart. He knows whether you are really wanting to serve Him or not, if you are struggling and sincerely seeking resolution. He knows if you want a clean slate. He knows if you have truly repented and He knows if you want to be forgiven.

So let's say you really have made a choice. But still you struggle! You might struggle with jealousy or envy, or an addiction. You might strike out in anger when you wish you hadn't. What to do? Like Joshua, we can say, "As for me and my house, we will serve the Lord." Still we struggle! What now? Honesty! Tell God how you feel. We can take the desire, the temptation to God. We can pray, telling God of our struggle. Some people try to hide their temptations and secret desires from God. He knows! He already knows and He wants to help us.

Let's look at an example. Perhaps you have been struggling with jealousy. It might be time to assess your belief about where your real value comes from. Jealousy is a sign that evil has already tricked you out of a blessing, the blessing that you are worthy. You can receive God's nurturing and care. You can go to Scripture and receive God's promise and care for you. Whatever our struggle, rather than just trying to get rid of it, we can ask God to teach us through the struggle. Isn't it ironic and interesting that evil and temptation leave us when we begin using the struggle they cause to deepen our relationship to God? Talk to God. He will listen and know and want to help you.

Remember God's commandments. God gave them to us in order to protect us. They are spiritual laws for living. Honesty brings its rewards. Dishonesty brings separation from God and from others. We can begin this day to head in the right direction, renewing our commitment and putting more of it into practice. Right now, we can commit to God. We can begin to practice our new behaviors. And when the struggle comes, as it might, we can talk to God about it, confiding in Him and asking His help. We can allow God to take two steps for us.

It is my prayer that each of us can allow God to take two steps for us, and that we can sense even more His presence with us, guiding, leading, loving and caring for us. Amen.

The choices we make every day reflect our ultimate choice.

The first line of this passage almost jumps out at us with its directive. "And now, O Israel, give heed to the statues and the ordinances which I teach you." A person who grew up being ordered around and receiving criticism and punishment might hear something negative implied in these words. You will be glad to know that this passage wants us to avoid hearing the words in any negative way. We are being told how important are the rules that God has given us, and how blessed we are for having them and living by them. This verse is signaling us to pay attention for our own safety and well-being. The statues and ordinances are God's commandments plus their elaboration. Deuteronomy gives us practical applications of how we can live with each other and with ourselves. There is deep wisdom in this book if you think of it as keeping you safe and healthy.

With the next words, we are told to follow the ordinances and statues so that we may live. This is like a loving mother telling us to stay out of the street, or to button up our coats, or to eat well—all so that we may be safe, and live our lives enjoyably and with meaning. We are told to pay heed to God's Words and to follow them. And there's more. Chapter 6: 6-7 says, "Keep these words that I am commanding you today in your heart. Recite them to your children and talk about them when you are home and when you are away, when you lie down and when you rise. Bind them as a sign on your hands, fix them as an emblem on your forehead, and write them on the doorposts of your house and on your gates."

As we're told here, we can let the wisdom of God's laws inform us and protect us. Then we can teach these things to our children and to each other. This will preserve us in our houses and when we go out into the world. In verse 2 we're told, "You shall not add to the word which I command you, nor take away from it, that you may keep the commandments of the Lord your God." This is to protect us from evil, which tries to influence us by adding to or taking away from what God actually commanded. Evil will alter what God really said so that following the commandments seems frustrating. We can end up "throwing the baby out with the bath water." We've all been tricked this way. One example: Evil implies that good people don't experience temptation. Then, by comparison, we come up short, get discouraged and give up. The truth is that everyone experiences temptation. It's human. Anytime we have rules we feel tempted to break them. But God tells us to keep the statutes and ordinances, to keep them in our hearts and minds. We can say them and place them in places where we will see them. This can help us with the temptations that come our way.

Evil tries also to convince us that God's laws are for God's benefit, not for ours, that God is just trying to keep us from the good stuff. The truth is that sin brings us pain, more sin, more pain, sickness and even death. God's way brings us forgiveness, a clean slate and a new start. We can get more health and happiness with God's blessings. We can experience inner peace and joy. Not really much of a comparison, is it?

When we read, study and know God's Word, we are filling our minds with God's thoughts. We bring God's Words into our hearts, minds, souls and spirit. We bring God's thoughts into our relationships, to the places where we travel, and to the people with whom we spend time. When we carry God's thoughts with us, we begin to change the way we think. We develop a secure foundation. Ultimately, meaning and purpose in our lives comes from our relationship to God. As we live with God's directives, we begin to see the love and deep care He has so lovingly laid out for us, the ways that He protects us and guides us to blessings. We are all here on Earth for such a short time. On our deathbeds, we'll want to be right with God. How wonderful to get right with God sooner, so that life can be lived with peace and happiness.

When we know the truth, it's so much easier for us. When we know the truth, we can follow God's path to a better life. We can be humble enough to ask for assistance. When we know God's Word, we can be wise enough to let God's Words calm the storm of our inner arguments. It is good and right to make peace in your heart by agreeing with God. Remember how relieved you have been when you have stopped warring with yourself over some sin. When you stopped and agreed with God's Word, remember how much more peace you felt.

Verse 6 says, "Keep them and do them, for that will be your wisdom and your understanding in the sight of others." We're given a shortcut to great wisdom and understanding! We don't have to unravel the mysteries of the universe, discover a new miracle drug or win the lottery. God's Word can give us great wisdom. After all, the Bible is the best book about psychology, the study of the mind. This is what God's Word offers us: an understanding of our minds. We get knowledge about our relationships, our inner selves, our families, our friends and the nations. We know more about being close to God and finding deep spiritual fulfillment.

It is my prayer that each of us can develop so much wisdom and understanding that others will begin to see where we got our insight, peace and joy. Amen.

We can develop the ability to choose well.

"Say to those who are of a fearful heart . . ." In Hebrew, a fearful person is one who makes hasty decisions. Snap decisions are not the best; often, they have gotten many of us in trouble. This is the kind of fear to which this passage refers, a kind of impatience and lack of ability to wait for the real blessing. A person in this state of fearfulness is anxious and restless in mind and soul. Who among us doesn't this address? Who among us has not sinned because we made hasty decisions? Who among us hasn't sinned because we were anxious and impatient? In essence, we lacked good sense and faith, and it led us to sin. Who among us hasn't wished that we had thought our way through a situation instead of acting immediately upon our feelings? The good news is that the Lord has encouragement for us! We can develop the ability to choose well so that we have good things instead of fear and regret.

The next words in this verse are, "Be strong, do not fear!" We might read this and think, "If only it was that easy." If only we could let go of our fear and anxiety. Most of us have tried to dispel our fears and worries by putting them away somewhere. We try not to think about them. But have you ever tried not to think about something" What happens? You think about it! If I told you not to think about red monkeys, what would happen? The moment you decide not to think about red monkeys, you think about them. You have to think about them first in order not to think about them next! So this isn't a very effective way of dealing with fear and worry.

Here, Scripture distinguishes between God's way and the world's way. God is telling us that it is possible for us to find our way to living from safety and security rather than fear. This passage tells us that the world's way of "just put it out of your mind" isn't going to work. God gives us a stern warning—a strong admonition—to avoid this kind of thinking. This is because every sin has fear at its base. If we want to avoid sin, then we'll need a new way of thinking about and dealing with fear.

Sin driven by fear takes many forms. Sometimes it looks like desire or want. Fear of being embarrassed is one that gets many of us. It may come across as a quest for approval. Fear of being lonely or rejected is another one that gets many of us. This fear may look like a need to keep people nearby all of the time or to maintain friendships that are not in our best interests. A fear of not being liked or accepted may be difficult to discern; it masks as an inability to say "no," a fear of hurting others' feelings, or an inability to stand up for ourselves. A fear of being looked down upon or being made fun of can lead people to lie. All of these fears can lead us to crazy decisions that we regret later.

Every commandment and every statute that a person breaks is broken out of fear or ignorance. Fear drives addicts to use drugs and dealers to sell them. Fear drives greed; if you fear that you are not enough without someone else's money or possessions, you will covet them. Then you will be tempted to try to take those things. When we sin, it is because we put fear first in our lives.

"Here is your God. He will come with vengeance, with terrible recompense of God. He will come and save you." In other words, God will fight against our fears if we will allow Him to. God will save us from our fears if we turn to Him. It's more than just asking God to take away our fears. God has given us a way that frees us! This is where our faith—a mustard seed of faith—comes in. God wants to save you from your fears. He wants you to feel protected and cared about. You may remember the song that says, "Oh, what peace we often forfeit, O what needless pain we bear all because we do not carry everything to Him in prayer."

When in the midst of our fears, if we turn our hearts and our lives over to God, a peace begins to accompany every breath we take. We feel that a weight has been lifted from our shoulders and we can relax. We feel comforted and can allow God to lead us to paths of righteousness. When we turn our will to God and give up those struggles, the fear diminishes and often disappears. We begin to feel a presence of care and compassion leading and directing us. Then the eyes of the blind will be opened and the ears of the deaf unstopped.

You might think of this as a miracle. All of us could tell of miracles we have experienced or seen. There are big ones and little ones. There are miracles of people overcoming histories of prostitution, of drug abuse or sickness. There are miracles of families being reunited, and parents and children being given another chance to know and love one another. There are miracles of people staying alive in spite of odds against them. It doesn't really matter if all kinds of worldly explanations are offered in these situations. We can see them through the eyes of faith. Throughout Scripture, we're told that in the face of miracles and revelations from God, fear not. In other words, have faith.

It is miraculous that we can pray, and feel comforted and important. It is miraculous that we can remember our own baptism, and feel clean and loved. It is a miracle when we receive communion and feel forgiven. It is my prayer that we can let go and let God open our eyes to the many miracles—and possibilities for them—in our lives, so that God can bless us even more. Amen.

You Can Be A World Class Learner
			Isa 50: 4-9, Mk 8: 27-35, Jas 2: 14-18

Morning by morning He awakens my ear . . .

Many of us have experienced grief and sadness. We can learn from these passages, noticing our mood improving as we hear uplifting and encouraging words.

The Lord gave Isaiah the tongue of a teacher, one who knew how to sustain the weary with words. Isaiah's wisdom and poetic language are legendary. His words are uplifting. Isaiah acknowledges that God gave him this gift. In so doing, Isaiah tells us that God's Words can sustain us. They can teach, comfort and guide us. They can be our companion and our friend, building us up. Isaiah must have been a very humble person in order to understand such great wisdom. He must have sought to learn from others so that he could develop wisdom. God doesn't just fill our heads with wisdom. We have to search it out and go after it in order to receive it. To really learn great things requires great humility, a learner's perspective on the world.

Arrogance, pride and stubbornness block learning. It is no wonder that people who are very arrogant or stubborn often make fools of themselves. They have closed themselves to learning. God lifts up the humble. Humility is the most self-respecting attitude you can adopt. It is also the healthiest. When we realize that God can (and often does) teach us through anyone—sometimes in surprising ways—we become eager to learn in a variety of circumstances. We are open to being taught things.

The verse, " . . . The Lord God has given me the tongue of a teacher that I may know how to sustain the weary with a word . . ." is more than poetic. It means that when we are willing to be taught—when we are humble—we can learn. When we seek after learning and present ourselves as willing to be taught, we open ourselves up to receiving the valuable and important lessons that change our lives. We can be sustained. This is why we say that humility is the greatest show of self-respect. Humility is required for any real growth and spiritual change.

This passage refers to Isaiah and also to world-class learners everywhere. By having a worshipful attitude that begins and ends with humility, we can allow God to help us develop an eagerness to learn. Learn best by putting away false pride and arrogance that act like they already know what's important. Admitting that we are powerless and empty enough to learn is how people develop the real ability to succeed. Some of us can say with Isaiah, "Morning by morning he wakens—wakens my ear to listen as those who are taught." Some of us are eager to learn. We seek out real wisdom and knowledge. Some of us can also say, "The Lord God has opened my ear and I was not rebellious, I did not turn backward." Some of us! Many of us at some time have rebelled and turned back and forth from real wisdom. But because we want to be faithful, we can take steps in the right direction. We can put away false pride and replace it with an inner knowing that we are important to God. We can let go of our indecision and then walk humbly with God. We can become true learners.

Verse 7 says, "The Lord God helps me; therefore I have set my face like flint, and I know that I shall not be put to shame." Most of us would like it if we never felt shame again. We would like to have a way of being safe, away from belittling words, put-downs, and negative, critical remarks. Perhaps the words that hurt the most have been echoing in our own heads, words that cut and hurt us since the first time they were said. You know the ones. We've all had people say things that seemed to cut right to the bone. Later, we kept hearing the words over and over. If this is so, perhaps it is time to allow God to help us let go of these things. One way is to discover how our false pride has kept us vulnerable to that hurt. When we really maintain our close relationship to God, letting go of false pride becomes easier and easier.

Proverbs says that pride goes before a fall. We can be humiliated only when we have allowed false pride to dominate our thoughts. How can someone make you feel humiliated if you are right with God? Who will contend with me? Who will fight with me? Who is my adversary? Let them come close because there is no fear. When we are willing to be taught and to learn, we have a humility that cannot be humiliated. Who will declare me guilty? When we let go of false pride and really draw on our relationship with God, we begin to have a real self-assurance. That is when others cannot hurt us. It can't stick, because we are defended with humility instead of false pride. A humble person cannot be humiliated!

Real humility begins with our awareness that we are less than God and that we can rely on His Word instead of our own logic. Putting ourselves above God is sin. Putting ourselves forward to learn from God is righteousness. Isaiah was a righteous person because he was willing to be wrong. He was willing to be taught, to seek out learning from the real source of all real knowledge and wisdom. He sought God's Word. As can we. We, too, can approach God with an empty cup by pouring out arrogance and false pride.

It is my prayer that each of us would seek God's guidance, using it as our measurement. May we accept even more eagerly God's blessings for our lives. Amen.

I'm on this journey. Come and walk with me.

The passage begins with, "It was the Lord who made it known to me, and I knew; then you showed me their evil deeds." When we begin to study the Bible and are seeking to do right, we become aware of other people's sins. We see plainly that they are violating God's laws. We can recognize their sinfulness and sometimes, their hypocrisy—when they say one thing and do another. There are even people whose sin we enjoy seeing because they have been so self-righteousness that seeing their mistakes makes us feel better. Sometimes, we see their sin in the words they choose, as when they profane a sacred name in order to sound dramatic. With some people, sin is in their gossip or their bragging about what they've done or are about to do. We see their tall tales for what they are; if these folks had the ability and determination to accomplish big things, would they really need to talk about them? You may even feel in your gut that what these people are doing is wrong and that you are right. You may have a slow-burning anger. You want them to stop doing what they are doing.

The next phase of our journey has gotten many people stuck. Like Jeremiah, we say, "But I was like a gentle lamb led to the slaughter. And I did not know it was against me that they devised schemes . . ." We imagine them saying about us, "Let us destroy the tree with its fruit, let us cut him off from the land of the living . . ." In this phase, we feel that others are trying to hurt or discredit us. We are aware of how unfair all of it seems. These people's actions may have begun when you really started to change. It seems that people who enjoy conflict sense spiritual change and don't like it. It is threatening to them. It's as though when you really make up your mind to get right with God, all hell breaks loose to come against you and tempt you. It may even seem that people went out of their way to make life difficult for you. Maybe it wasn't people, but events that seemed to pile up on you, one after another. When this happens, it could only be evil trying to dissuade you from having a genuine commitment to God.

Like Jeremiah, we know that God's judgment will be fair. In times like these, even when we grow out of seeking vengeance ourselves, we may ask God to levy it. We pray, like Jeremiah, to see God's vengeance on our enemies. "But you, O Lord of hosts, who judge righteously, who try the heart and the mind. . . ." We want God with us. We want Him to protect us and sometimes, we want to see that the people who hurt us get what we think they deserve: God's vengeance. Jeremiah prayed for this in verse 20. So did the psalmist—over and over.

Somehow, like Jeremiah and like the psalmist, we forget that we, too, are sinners. We, too, have hurt others. We may have lied or cheated or stolen. We may have betrayed someone. We may have done some of the things that were done to us. We all have sinned and, whether we know it or not, our sin hurt others. We may even have hurt loved ones and made it more difficult for them to trust us. They may have forgiven us, but still, we may have driven a wedge into the heart of the relationship. Our sin affects our children. Of course it does. In Deuteronomy 4:9, God's Word says that the sins of the mothers and fathers would be visited upon the children to the third and fourth generations. Our sin affects people. Sometimes, addicts believe that they hid their addiction from their children. Do they really think that their children don't know? That they are unaffected? Unless cleansed by faith, our sin travels through us to others, even from generation to generation.

Somewhere along our path, we realize that we, too, need forgiveness. We, too, need a pardon. We, too, need to feel like we are cleaning up the messes we have made. When we can acknowledge that we also need forgiveness from God and from our loved ones, it is easier for us to let go of our anger toward other people. We can realize that we have progressed from the point of being near-sighted about other people's sins to being far-sighted about God's love for them and for us.

Throughout the Bible, we are encouraged, challenged, chastised and warned to repent. When we are really in touch with our need for forgiveness, we *want* to repent. We want to be able to be proud of ourselves and to know that God's face is shining down on us with pleasure at our growth. When we repent and turn back from sin, God rejoices. By beginning today, we can change our future and its effects on our own lives and the lives of others. As Joshua 24:15 says, "Choose you this day whom you will serve." And, like him, we can say," As for me and my house, we will serve the Lord." We can begin today.

I'm on this journey. Come and walk with me. We can do what we know we ought to do. We can make amends. We can invite the Lord's direction. We can lean on His understanding. We can forgive and we can ask for forgiveness. We can repent. We all know some of the ways that the Lord has been talking to us about our behavior. We know some of the changes that He expects. I don't know them for you, but you do. If your denial is too high, then ask God to reveal them to you.

It is my prayer that each of us will let our God come on, walk with us and clean us up so that we can hold our heads up high and know that He is on the journey with us. Amen.

Volunteering to do good things brings positive changes in you.

Moses was completely overwhelmed by the task facing him until God spoke to him through his father-in-law. This is an important life lesson. Sooner or later, we all realize that we need help. We find out that we do have limits, that we are not so independent, and that we need others. We are *interdependent.* We can learn from Moses, that mighty leader and spiritual giant. Moses was humble enough to ask for help. That's not always easy, is it? Initially, Moses resisted asking for help for many of the same reasons that we do. He liked feeling important. He did not want to let go of the feeling he had of being very important to and needed by his people.

Perhaps, too, Moses did not want to face his limits. Interestingly, our limits—our weaknesses—are the places where we have the most opportunity for spiritual growth. It's reassuring to think of a weakness in this way. It changes from something we fear to something we can embrace. Moses did this. He came around, realizing that in recognizing his needs, he acknowledged his importance. In this way, his humility was an indication of his self-respect. When we ask for help, it is also a sign of our self-respect. It is only when we are honest with ourselves about our need for help that we can begin to receive it.

Isn't it a bit ironic that when we ask for help we are helping others too? You may have struggled to ask for help. Maybe you even asked in an obscure way, hoping that someone would read your mind and know that you were needful. Yet you remember the times when someone has asked your opinion or asked you for encouragement. You felt honored. Your friend or associate respected you enough to ask your opinion about some matter. They were asking you to share your wisdom or your experience with them. It feels good, doesn't it?

What keeps us from giving more to each other in this way? Just as God worked through the people of the Bible, God works for others through us. Maybe God encouraged you through someone's kind word or guidance, or through an invitation to church or Bible study or another spiritual place. Looking over your life, you know that not only has God loved you, but others have, too. A good friend of mine says that real love is taking obvious pleasure in another's happiness. That takes all the guesswork out of it, doesn't it?

When you reach out for someone, you demonstrate acceptance, forgiveness and perhaps even *agape*—the biggest love, God's love of us that we can show to others. God wants us to recognize this kind of love.

He wants to work through you. He wants us to love one another as we love ourselves. He wants us to show kindness to others and kindness to ourselves. When you realize that you are a pipeline for God's love to another person, you will experience an amazing feeling. It is an awesome realization. God wants to work through you for others.

All spiritual truths come from God. It doesn't matter what denomination or faith group we're dealing with. All spiritual truth comes from the same source. Often, you have known this. You've had that special knowing inside that something was deeply and completely true. It may have been a truth that resonated through your entire being. You felt peaceful in knowing this truth. The more you find yourself in tune with God, the more in tune with Him you want to be. The more you want to be close to God, the closer to Him you will be.

When we are interested in finding the truth, we can know that it will always be reflected in the Bible. The Bible can teach us the most when we are looking for the expression of its truths in our lives. For example, we know intellectually that God loves us. Yet how much more we can feel God's love when other believers care for us and show us that love. This is how the Bible can affect us most powerfully: through the caring of others.

Our faith is the key. It opens the door for us to give and receive blessings. It is always through faith that God works to heal, to help, to console, to bind up and to save. And our faith gets stronger with use. It is just like muscles, talents and abilities. The more you use them, the stronger they get. The stronger your faith gets, the more you are blessed, and the more you can give and receive. As James 2:18 says, " . . . You have faith and I have works. Show me your faith apart from your works and I by my works will show you my faith." This is how we help express God's love in the world.

Put your faith to work. Imagine what would happen if every one of us began to perform a few more acts of kindness than we normally would do. Can you imagine how much fun it would be to watch people who don't like us very much when we're kind to them? They might even begin to change! Just because God wants to work through you doesn't mean it can't be fun! Will you meet my challenge to do at least one additional kind thing today?

It is my prayer that all of us will recognize how much God depends on us to express His love for us through each other. I also pray that as we do, we will recognize a little more of how much God loves us and wants good things for us this day and every day. Amen.

Letting Go Of Blame
Mk 10: 2-16, Gen 2:18-24, Heb 2: 9-13

When we bless others, we get blessed, too.

It would be easy to think that this passage is about divorce, remarriage and adultery. It would be easy to misunderstand it, and to interpret it as strict, harsh and unforgiving. Nothing could be father from the truth. Let's allow God's Spirit to touch our hearts and minds this day with what will help us to become better believers and people.

Verse 2 reads, "Some Pharisees came and to test him, they asked . . ." Right from the beginning, the Pharisees had an accusatory attitude toward Jesus. They had already decided that they were against him. Because their attitude toward him was both judgmental and condemning, they wanted either to shame him publicly or to trick him. They had no forgiveness and no love in their hearts. They were too busy blaming people. People who feel blame have a tendency to blame. Sometimes it is a desperate feeling of fear that leads them to this; if they don't put the blame on someone else, it might stick to them!

In most families, there is a blaming process. If something breaks or stops working, blame is often assigned to someone in the family. The item may have been twelve years old and completely worn out, but woe to the person who was using it when it broke! You know how it is. The feeling then is to avoid blame and so, we blame the problem on someone else. We all feel and do these things sometimes. But where real faith lives, there is no need for blame. When we know and live with forgiveness, we realize that making mistakes is part of living. We feel no need to blame others. We know that it serves no purpose. The Bible is about forgiveness and discovering that we are important. The Bible gives us laws and rules in order to protect and guide us to fulfilling lives in relationship to God. When we have real faith, blame falls by the wayside.

The Pharisees taunted Jesus with a trick question. It was a public ambush. They wanted him to answer in a way that they could use against him. If they could get Jesus to say either that divorce should be easier or that it should be rejected entirely, his popularity would suffer. The Pharisees' belittling attitude rejects God. That legalistic, judgmental stance that some people adopt is against God. They imply that because they know best, they don't need God. When we condemn others, where is our own acknowledgement of our sin? Where is our own need for forgiveness? We've all known someone like the Pharisees: a prune-faced, legalistic, critical person who is busy finding fault with others. In fact, many of us have that person living in our own heads! This makes us feel shame and that we are lesser than others. We may even have blamed others to try to get relief from the shame that we felt.

The entire conversation with Jesus in this passage was about someone trying to trick him. In Jesus' day, divorce was something that only men could do. Women were not allowed to divorce their husbands. Generally, women were treated very badly. The Pharisees' attitude was used to justify men divorcing their wives and leaving them very badly off. Jesus countered this. And then he did something else radical. He put women on an equal footing with men, by saying, " . . . And if she divorces her husband and marries another . . ." Can you imagine? Jesus turned the Pharisees' world upside down and exposed their prejudice. They must have been shocked and even confused.

When people interpret this passage legalistically and condemn divorced people, they are forgetting John 3:17, which reads," . . . God did not send the Son into the world to condemn the world, but in order that the world might be saved through him." And verse 18, which says," Those who believe in him are not condemned."

Next we see the disciples trying to protect Jesus by keeping the children in a crowd away from him. The crowd had gathered to hear him speak. Perhaps Jesus was tired. No doubt the disciples meant well, but Jesus speaks up and says, "Let the children come to me. Do not hinder them for it is to such as these that the kingdom of God belongs." Jesus' correction of his disciples was loving. This kind of correction makes you want to accept your own mistakes and even rejoice when they are brought to your attention! And isn't this different from the attitude of the Pharisees? When we know that God loves us, we know that a loving correction shows that we are cared about.

Verse 15 reads, "Truly, I tell you, whoever does not receive the kingdom of God like a little child will never enter it." Do you remember your own childlike wonder at the world? How you looked forward to learning? How accepting of love you were as a child? Verse 16 is so comforting. It says, "And he took them up in his arms and laid his hands on them and blessed them." You can close your eyes for a moment and feel the sincerity of Jesus in his caring for you. You can imagine him putting his hand on your head and saying to you something like, "You are my child in whom I am well pleased. May God's love and protection stay with you day after day and all the rest of your life." It's kind of nice to understand Scripture in a personal way like that, isn't it?

It is prayer that you will continue to receive God's Word in this way. Amen.

Wisdom is a by-product of faith, love and knowledge.

This passage from Scripture begins with," Happy are those who find wisdom and those who get understanding." In the Bible, wisdom and understanding are distinctly different, even though we tend to use the words interchangeably. Understanding is perhaps best defined as discernment. Discernment makes some of our hunches more powerful, because discernment relies on God's Word and orients our intuitions. Understanding is a gift because in order to have it, we must be honest with ourselves and with God.

Wisdom is intertwined with faith in God. It comes as a gift to believers. It is given to us at the spiritual level and when we follow God's laws. One wise person said, "Wisdom is a philosophy of life rooted in the soil of life." It is a practical approach to our challenges and difficulties that is based on successful tried-and-tested approaches. Proverbs 1:7 reads," The beginning of wisdom is the fear of the Lord." Faith in God is foundational to wisdom. Without faith, all that a person can achieve is knowledge. This person may be cunning and shrewd but he or she will not be wise. Wisdom is more than gathering facts and using them for self-promotion. It is a by-product of faith, love and knowledge.

Human culture has valued things like gold and jewels. They've been bought and sold, coveted, stolen, hoarded and fought over. Our paper money is based on the gold standard. But as much value as these things have for many people, they do not come close to what we gain when we have wisdom. It is so much better than gold. The wisdom you already have from your faith and your knowledge of the Bible is valuable. Most of us have more of it than we realize, and we rely on it a good bit of the time. The more we recognize that our wisdom comes from our faith and our study of Scripture, the more we can take a genuine pride in it at the same time that we have a humble and thankful attitude. And isn't it interesting that the more you give your wisdom away, the more it is really yours?

This passage portrays wisdom as a woman whose gift is precious far beyond gold or jewels. This woman named wisdom gives long life in her right hand and riches and honor in her left. This is something that our culture often ignores. How likely is it that we would find a newspaper headline, "Woman Achieves Wealth and Respect Over Time by Applying Principles From the Bible"? One of the most encouraging things to me that my denomination does is to publish the obituaries of ministers. I find often that these people have lived longer than average life spans. These paragraphs describe the lives of those who had faith and who sought wisdom.

Verse 15 says that nothing else you desire can compete with this woman of wisdom. Wisdom is more valuable than worldly possessions or popularity. It's better than someone telling you that you are this or that wonderful thing. It's better than a flashy car or control or worldly power. When you are wise, people begin to see that your word counts.

On the other hand, worldly savvy is about "getting over." It's slick. It's about gaining control over people, about getting from them everything that can be taken. Worldly pretenders worry about getting caught. They manipulate people and use them. Their approach is boastful, fleshy and ends in destruction. They reap what they sow. Suspicion, loneliness and lack of trust echo throughout their lives. God's wisdom is based on our loving God and seeing our neighbors as ourselves. No one can really lay claim to loving God unless they are willing to love their neighbor. You may not like your neighbor, but loving him or her means that you want good for them. What comes from this approach to life are honor, peace, long life and a sense of being cared about.

The way society looks at God's wisdom and those who receive it hasn't changed much, really. In Jeremiah's time, some wanted wisdom and some just wanted to "get over." In David's day, some people really valued wisdom. Some said they did but never sought to learn from God's Word. It has been the same throughout all of the centuries.

God's wisdom is given to us in His rules and laws. They are the direction we receive in the Bible. Putting into practice more of what we read, study and learn protects us and brings us peace and happiness. Remember a time when you stopped rebelling against God's law and accepted it? Remember how much peace you felt as you acknowledged your sin and asked for forgiveness? You may be advanced enough in your faith to be able to receive a peaceful feeling, and a sense of being loved and of having a friend every time you read Scripture. Most of the time, I do. I carry a Bible with me so that I can have that calm, peaceful feeling of rest any time that I might need or want it. I like how reading the Bible gives me a feeling of being loved and cared about. I enjoy that feeling of closeness to God, and of feeling cared about through His words speaking to me. Many of you enjoy this feeling, too.

So let your light shine through. Allow others to see your faith and the wisdom that you have been given by God. Show your courage by demonstrating some more of that wisdom by giving thought to how often, where and when you seek out God's Word. And demonstrate your wisdom by showing your ability to love your neighbor. This is my prayer. Amen.

39

What About The Tough Times?
Isa 53: 10-12, Mk 10: 35-45, Heb 5: 1-10

Some words come to life. Some words bring life.

This passage from Isaiah is part of a famous one called "The Suffering Servant." We can learn from it if we allow ourselves to pray that God will bring what is useful and healing to our hearts and minds. One way we can understand Scripture is first to realize that it is always speaking of stories and people of ancient times. Then we can remember that Scripture also shows us positive and negative role models. Scripture is always speaking to us about our own lives. God's Word is alive and active.

Verse 10 says it was the Lord's will to "crush him with pain." Of whom does Isaiah speak? Some people say this refers only to Jesus, but many people found comfort in this passage long before Jesus' time. "Comfort!" you snort. "Where is the comfort in God crushing someone with pain?" It is a difficult question, one central to the development of faith. How can God be a good God who loves us yet allows our suffering?

Down through the ages many believers have read Isaiah's words and have known that they applied. Believers have been crushed right along with non-believers. As Job said, "Pain and suffering fall on the just and the unjust." Perhaps the importance lies in how people handle misfortune. Often, after suffering, believers will thrive. They get stronger emotionally. They become more spiritually attuned and receive multiple blessings for their efforts. They have the lasting satisfaction of knowing that their lives resemble daily sermons that give others hope, health and honesty. Non-believers have allowed bitterness and anger to consume them. They have been tricked by evil into losing sight of the source of their help.

This passage—and ones like it—spoke to many people who suffered through World War II and the Holocaust: people who watched their loved ones killed; people who were tortured and starved; and people who were taken from their homelands and turned into slaves. They knew intimately the words of the suffering servant. Yet some of them, despite their tragedies and extreme pain, were not completely torn apart. They became stronger. Their struggles were very, very difficult. But, in the end, they triumphed through faith and they let that faith shine through.

I know a woman who suffered through a difficult childhood. Her mother was very busy with routine tasks and did not pay much attention to her daughter, who became increasingly lonely. No one seemed to notice that the girl's brother picked on her. No one seemed to care that he hurt her. And then one day the little girl's brother did the unthinkable. He forced himself upon her. She sank into feeling dirty, violated and ashamed. Filled with despair and deeply alone, she kept the incident—and her feelings—to herself. One crisis after another hit the family. Over the years, the young woman buried her feelings and went on. She always hoped that somehow God would make things right but she suffered mightily.

This woman is grown now. Over time and with help, she has been able to let go of the feelings of shame and to feel cleansed by God. Reminders of her abuse no longer crush her. Today, she can point to her own healing as testimony of God's grace, power and love. Today, she is able to reach out to others who still are feeling the anguish of shame and past hurts. She helps them see their worth and value. You can see her light shine through her actions and you can feel her faith in her determination to remain as true to God as possible. She knows that her faith sustains her.

When I read verses 11 and 12 about the suffering of his soul and that through his righteousness he will be a great help to many and counted among the great, I remember that through his faith, even Abraham's sin became righteousness. I am reminded of a woman who struggled valiantly against the cruelty of beatings, sacrificing herself to protect her children from similar beatings. I am reminded of a woman of faith who prayed for years for her long lost child. She wondered, "Does anyone care for her? Is she warm? Is she safe? Is she loved?" The light of this woman's faith and love gave her hope. She gave hope to others, too. And, happily, there was a reunion of mother and child.

I know people who hold out hope for many things. Their faith is a light to others. I also know men and women who would never think of themselves as able to triumph over suffering. Their self-esteem is so low that they feel they deserve pain and anguish. They feel guilt, remorse and genuine repentance. But they are unable to see that they are a light to others. Of course, all of us have sinned. It is what we do with that sin that matters the most. The great believers kept their own sins present in their minds; it helped them to remember how good God was to forgive them and to aid them in overcoming their past transgressions. Many would even boast about what God had done to clean their hearts and lead them to righteous behavior.

If you let yourself, you can see the light in many people's faith. You can see their belief in their hope. You can see their righteousness in their healing and change. Some people have found the love and affection they sought from parents or children or friends. Some have found that affection in new parent figures and in new friends. Giants of faith show love and devotion daily. This passage calls for us to look at our own lives and to lean more on God. It is my prayer that each of us will allow God's Word to touch and to bless us. Amen.

40

Looking Through Positive Eyes
Jer 31: 7-9, Heb 5:1-6, Mk 10: 46-52

Joy is a choice for living.

This passage reads, "For thus says the Lord: Sing aloud with gladness for Jacob, and raise shouts for the chief of the nations . . ." In other words, we are to be joyful. (The words glad and joy in Hebrew are similar.) Psalm 100 says, "Make a joyful noise to the Lord, all the earth. Worship the Lord with gladness; come into his presence with singing . . ." If God wants us to be glad or joyful, there must be a reason. I trust that what God asks of us is possible.

A while back, I was confronted by this passage and also by a friend of mine. (When God tells us something through two or three sources, it is time to listen!) My friend said to me," . . . you love the Lord. . . . show it! Let your joy show. Be glad!" It had never occurred to me before that these references in the Bible meant that I personally was to be joyful. A little puzzled, I decided to understand this "joy thing" better.

I want to confess to you that the idea of joy and its manifestation are difficult concepts. But there is great wisdom in the concept of joy. For instance, Nehemiah 8: 10 says, ". . . . the joy of the Lord is your strength." For all of us who have been praying for strength, here is how we find it. Our joy of the Lord is our strength. When we increase our joy, we increase our strength. We can't force joy. But *we can choose it.* We can surrender into God's serenity and joy.

Joyful praise of the Lord is our strength. What a wonderful idea. As we choose to praise God with an attitude of gladness and joy, we find our way to strength. To increase our strength, we can simply increase our praise with more joy and gladness.

That said, one of the things I have learned is that gladness and joy do not come to us like rain falling from the sky. We must go out and search for them. We need to choose joy intentionally. We need to work at the process. Recently, I helped a teenager find something positive in what authority figures said to him even when they were correcting him. He is very bright and after a bit, he challenged me. "Okay, what is so positive in 'Shut up, James'?" The phrase "shut up" is very negative to me, so much so that I avoid its use. So I felt very challenged by his question! After a while, though, it came to me. How we take a comment from someone else is up to us. It is *our* choice. So I said, "It means that I like you enough to be unprofessional and personal with you the way I might be with someone in my family." We can praise God by choosing to think about the things in our lives that make us feel good. We can choose to focus on these things.

Psalm 32:11 says, "Be glad in the Lord and rejoice, O righteous, and shout for joy, all you upright in heart." During any given day, there are sights and sounds that could produce bad feelings, sadness or a lack of hope in any of us. We could dwell on what did or did not happen, or on what wasn't right in the past. We could focus on what we didn't have or couldn't have or never will have. We could make ourselves quite miserable. Or we can choose to find and dwell upon what the apostle Paul called," . . . whatever is true, whatever is just, whatever is pure, whatever is lovely, whatever is gracious. If there is any excellence, if there is anything worthy of praise, think about these things."

You might be thinking," But I don't feel like it!" or "I know they didn't mean anything good by what they said to me" or "I have plenty of reason to feel badly!" Well, here's a question for you. Who said that that was the only choice before you? Our feelings follow from what we have chosen to think about. Isaiah 12:3 reads, "With joy you will draw water from the wells of salvation." Joy is the cup from which we receive salvation. When we choose a joyful attitude, we are choosing to place ourselves in a position of righteous attitude from where we can be blessed by God. You talk about the Living Water! Tears of joy and shivers of realization can go up and down your spine as you live in daily search of the manna from Heaven we are already given: a daily bread of joy.

A woman of real faith and joy whom I know could easily have chosen to live in sadness and misery She has had a double mastectomy, a hysterectomy and other surgery for cancer. She is young and has no children. Yet in her presence you feel her enthusiasm for living. It is infectious. She chooses to find joy in her life. I know that God must admire her courage to choose joy. It seems to me that to choose joy one must be very deliberate in what one chooses to focus on. In some ways, it's the opposite of being controlled by our day-to-day wants and desires.

God confronted me through Scripture and through my friend. I was challenged to find more joy in my life. Passing on to you what has been given to me, I challenge you, too. Commit yourself to finding the things that are right, just, excellent, lovely, gracious and true. Dwell on these things. Search for these things. Admire these things. Then, try finding what is gracious and lovely in people you don't like. It will change how you feel when you see them. It might not change them but it will change you. It will give you joy.

It is my prayer that each of us can bring each other more joy by finding, dwelling upon and giving away more of God's joy this day and every day. Amen.

41

Falling In Love With God
Deut 6:1-9, Heb 7:23-28, Mk 12:28-34

"You shall . . ." may be prophecy . . .

This passage from Deuteronomy is a very famous one. There is so much wisdom packed into it that we could study it for an entire month and not get all that it has to offer. Would you pray with me that God speaks to you through these words, letting your spirit receive what it needs today?

I am excited about what I hear in this passage. God wants us to be lovers! God wants us to be in love with Him so that He can bless us. He wants us to be close to Him, to love Him with all our heart, with all our soul and with all our might. This passage says, "You shall love the Lord your God. . . ." *You shall.* Some might read a command into this phrase—and then rebel against it! They might feel disrespected by someone ordering them to do something. Perhaps, though, you could think of "you shall . . ." as a prophecy, that you are heading toward a closer relationship with God.

The people who really serve the Lord are in love with God and feel loved by God. There's a big difference between loving God and trying to obey God without loving Him. We are told that God's people shall love Him. So just how does this happen? Are we to wait for a lightening bolt to strike us and then we'll love God? In part, it means realizing that God already loves us and wants to bless us. It means realizing that God wants to have a relationship with us that is so satisfying that our feelings of loneliness dissipate.

Through faith, we are to accept God's love of us and allow it to transform us. Love is given and can only be given. It is never forced. To accept this means to become deeply involved with God. When we are deeply in love, everything else becomes secondary. When we are deeply in love, we think about our loved one. We want to tell others about the relationship. We enjoy simply thinking about our loved one. This is the way God feels about us. As our parent, God loves us so much that He tells us the secret to happiness and a long life. The more we love God, the more we are changed by love, by that bond between us.

When we love someone and trust that they love us back, we want reminders of them around us. We want things that bring back to us our connection to them, sentimental reminders like letters and photographs. We want to keep that sense of connection in the front of our minds because it is so fulfilling. When we love God and feel close to God, we will want these reminders of His love on a daily basis, before us and in the center of our vision always. When we love this much, God will be our sister, brother, mother and father. We will feel His presence always and everywhere, and we will never feel alone because our best friend is with us. And, as Deuteronomy tells us, we will want to teach our children about God, about His acceptance, and about how He knows everything about us and loves and wants us still.

Many of us are on our way. I have times when I feel God's love so powerfully that I just want to tell someone. To move closer to God means first knowing that it can happen. Then we can make decisions that move us closer each day. Each day that we get up searching for how God will speak to us can be an exciting day. It can also deepen the relationship significantly.

Not too long ago, at a meeting of several chaplains, I sat next to the one who was going to lead the devotion. After prayer, he began to share with us where in Scripture the Lord had been talking to him. With tears in his eyes, he spoke of how grateful he was to God for showing him how he could improve his love of God. He shared with us his sense that God had stepped on his toes a little bit to correct him in something he was doing. As I looked around at the other chaplains, I knew that God had spoken to this man and was now speaking to us through him. At first I felt little smug, thinking, "Yeah, God's really telling them that they need to improve." I wanted to exclude myself. Then I caught a glance of the chaplain's Bible. It was filled with notes and references. Passages were highlighted and underlined. Clearly, the man had studied his Bible extensively and was carrying reminders of God's love with him. I felt humbled! I still don't write in my Bible; it just isn't me. But I left the meeting that day with new conviction. I studied the passages the man had quoted. And I determined that in my own way, I would continue to let others see how I love God.

I thank God for showing me things through that experience. Like many of you, I carry with me reminders of my relationship to God. Each time that we choose to go to Him for guidance, to choose to feel close to Him and to feel His love, we set the stage for more in the future.

When we love God with all of our heart, we will talk about God's statutes when we sin. We will commit to a loving relationship to Him when we walk and when we lie down and when we get up. We will do it because our cup is near to running over and because we feel anointed to tell others how much God is doing for us.

It is my prayer that each of us will let ourselves feel God's love for us, and let it transform us even more, so that we can be a blessing to others as well. Amen.

42

Hearing the Call
1 Kings 17: 8-16, Heb 9:24-28, Mk 12:38-44

What we focus on will tell us a lot about where we are going.

On the surface, this story is about a miracle. It's easy when reading about some of the miracles in the Bible to discount them, especially because of the way many of them are written with a matter-of-fact tone. Sometimes, the level of faith displayed in them is so far removed from our own experience that we tend to start feeling demoralized, wondering why we don't have that much faith. In this story, we might find ourselves wondering if the widow was honest about how much oil and meal she really had. Did God miraculously keep refilling the oil and meal jars? Had the widow pessimistically underestimated how much she had? Was the miracle one of sharing? Did other people donate food because of Elijah?

Elijah had been alone in the wilderness and was destitute. He had nothing—no food, water or companionship. Surely, he had few options available to him when God told him to go to Zarephath, where a widow would take care of him. When you are hungry and thirsty—you have nothing left—and God tells you to go somewhere, it can be easy to hear the call. Sometimes, we are so stubborn that we have to get this desperate. Following God has to be our only option before we will let God lead us. Elijah had two options: He could die or he could allow God to lead him.

One of the messages of this passage is about responsiveness to God. At first, Elijah and the widow had very few options. Then they were both responsive to God. I find this encouraging for us. When most of us come to God, we have very few options left either. Elijah seemed to be on a training path. And God fed him in the wilderness

God told Elijah and the widow about each other and they listened. Each of them had at least a little hope left and was willing to give God leadership in their lives. They were willing to respond to God's direction. This is different from being compliant. We might comply with what someone in a position of authority tells us to do while we question it internally. When we are responsive, we are active. We want to *do* something. For example, when we know that someone we trust really cares about us, we are responsive to their suggestions.

Elijah, that giant of faith, left the brook when it dried up and God told him to go. He headed out in search of the widow. In our faith journey, we are first responsive to God when the brook dries up, when we have no other options. Then it gets easier, as we begin to get closer to Him and realize that what He wants from us really is in our best interest. It gets easier still when we develop a daily relationship with Him.

As it was for Elijah and the widow, it is important for us to reach that place by trusting God on a daily basis and sharing our faith with one other person. This miracle wasn't just about getting Elijah fed. It was not just about getting the widow and her son fed. It wasn't even about getting them all fed together. It was about getting people of faith to help one another.

This is one law about how our minds work: What we put our faith in is what we will head for. When our outlook is bleak and we see only doom and gloom, that's where we're headed. The widow saw only death and hopelessness at first. She was planning to have her last meal with her son and then die. Her lack of hope and her preoccupation with her fears were heading her for destruction. Elijah, on the other hand, had begun to believe that when God dried up one opportunity, another would appear if Elijah went in search of it. Our faith is a powerful force that is taking us toward either destruction or toward blessings.

Throughout the Bible, we're encouraged to trust in God's desire to bless us. The temptation is always there to look at how little we have, to anticipate destruction. But when we go in search of God's blessings, we can find them. They aren't always where we thought they'd be, but we will find them. Evil tries to steal our hope by tricking us into dwelling on what we do not have. We can be so tricked that we hear only criticism, prejudice and rejection, even when it's not there.

On the other hand, we can look for the blessing in our difficulties. I remember one week at the prison where several people misinterpreted something I had said. I might have said, "Woe is me. Why does this always happen?" And that temptation was there, believe me. But rather, I said to myself, "Somewhere in those misunderstandings there is a potential blessing for me and for those other people. I'm going in search of it." I thought that perhaps God was showing me that the brook of how I had been doing something was drying up, and I needed to go in search of new ways of relating in an institution that was changing.

God is speaking to all of us. There are always changes around us. There are changes in the world, in our country and in our families. There are changes in the people around us at work. There are changes in us. Even if we have been seeing only doom and gloom around us, even if we have been seeing only through eyes of fear, the Lord is speaking to us. We can support each other. We can let others see our faith. In so doing, we continue to be responsive to God's call.

It is my prayer that each of us will hear God's call and listen for the ways in which He is encouraging us to change and to reach out and help one another. Amen.

Blessings are gifts received.

Why does the Bible always seem to offer a promise of reward for righteousness and a threat for sin? This is a big question. How we live with it makes all the difference in the world. Let us pray that we will hear what the Lord has to say to us.

When I was younger, whenever I heard preachers use a "carrot and stick" approach of reward and punishment, it left me uneasy. I felt manipulated and didn't like it at all. So I won't do that to you. Instead, let me say this: Every decision that we make in life offers us a possible reward or punishment. Most of us want to know how we are doing. Daniel gives us reassurance that all whose names are written in the Book shall be delivered, delivered like a new baby, innocent and wanted. Isn't that a nice idea that we can be delivered to a new birth, toward reward and away from punishment?

I have a friend who is a pilot. I know that the way that pilots learn to fly a steady course is to pick out an object on the horizon and fly toward it. Rather than worry about every small deviation from course, they set their eyes on their goal and use this to guide them. Of course, we are not learning to fly. . . . or are we? Isn't it true that we are learning how to chart our own course in our earthly and spiritual lives?

Shame is something that all of us have felt at one time or another. It's not a good feeling! It feels like a bone-deep humiliation. Being left feeling shame forever would be quite a punishment, indeed. Shame in our lives can leave us feeling deeply lonely. Some people feel shame from past abuse or from sin. People who are healing from past shame often notice how easy it is to have the shame surface again and again. Sometimes fear triggers it. For some, remembering feelings of grief or sadness can also trigger shame and the feeling that they are not enough. Some people find that shame follows feelings of anger.

Each time that we encounter these feelings of fear or shame from the past, we have an opportunity to let our faith lead us. Each time is an opportunity to reaffirm our faith. This is one place where we can get a reward. Instead of repeating the old patterns of fear, shame, anger, sadness and hopelessness, we can look to our faith to lead us to a new place of opportunity for growth.

Ephesians 5:13-14 reads, " . . . everything exposed by the light becomes visible, for everything that becomes visible is light . . ." I have worked with many people who were healing from past shame. They got to the point in their journeys where they saw that God had touched their lives. They could testify in front of others that they had been able to face shameful events from their pasts and face what they had done. They were able to realize that they were forgiven, and they became powerful witnesses to the awesomeness and goodness of God's grace. This was reward.

This passage in Daniel says, "Those who are wise shall shine like the brightness of the sky, and those who turn many to righteousness, like the stars forever and ever." Each time we demonstrate our faith by acting on it, we burn brighter. Each time we help others to turn to faith and righteousness, we burn even brighter. We do this best by living with our faith very present. This means that we have taken responsibility for our pasts and have been admitting what we have really experienced. It's about going toward our fears so they don't have power over us.

Someone told me a story about a seven-year boy who demonstrated this beautifully. At school, a girl was picking on him. Then she invited all of the children in her class except this little boy to her birthday party. He felt left out and humiliated. Do you know what he did? He went up to the girl, tapped her on the shoulder and told her that he would like to go to her party, too. Would she please invite him? Shocked, she told him she would think about it and ask her mother. Guess what? The little boy was invited—and the girl stopped picking on him. He moved toward his fears and feelings of shame, and he got a reward.

Facing our fears is an affirmation of faith. It's a way of flying toward our goal rather than away from what we don't want. Our reward will be good, affirming feelings that will help us have more health, more faith and a brighter future. "Those who are wise will shine like the brightness of the sky, and those who turn many to righteousness like the stars forever and ever." What has helped you to change? Who helped you to turn? Was it someone believing in you and showing you that it could be done? Someone who showed you that you can walk by faith rather than familiarity?

Daniel reads, " . . . at that time your people shall be delivered, everyone who is found written in the book." Through faith, we stake our claim to be written in the Book. If we want an invitation, all we have to do is ask. If we want to be included, we can focus on our goal. We have to keep our eyes on where we want to go.

It is my prayer that every shred of shame and fear in our lives becomes evidence of God's power to transform, of what God is doing and how God is working through us. I pray also that we encourage others to follow Him as well. Now I know you know how to answer the big question. Amen.

Your "spirit part" knows.

This passage is about a dream that Daniel had. Though we haven't always known how to interpret them, we've all had dreams that we felt meant something. There are some major truths about interpreting signs and messages from God in this passage. Will you pray with me that each of us will get better at understanding messages we receive from God? Let us pray that the spiritual part of each of us connects with God's Spirit.

What this passage implies is that the God of creation is a God who will demonstrate his awesome power at the end of time and establish his kingdom forever. We've all heard people who claim to have a pipeline to God predicting the end of time. But God will give to all who are willing to understand. Some of us may have been given a greater ability to understand and teach Scripture or even to prophesy, but the truth is, God's truths are open to all who are willing to receive them. The real prophets were open to hearing God speaking to them. They were not advancing themselves. They were bringing to us messages of how we need to straighten our paths and change our ways because of sin. Real prophecy is concerned with our being saved by living right with God. Real prophets care about much more than their image. They are humble about their gifts and bold about what God is doing.

All around us are radio waves being broadcast by various radio stations. To receive the sound, we need to have a receiver that is tuned to a particular frequency. This is a good metaphor for how we can hear God speaking to us. Is your receiver tuned in? Think of it this way: We have a spirit part and a flesh part. Your spirit part can know something even if your flesh part doesn't realize it. Your spirit part can know when God is speaking to you. In fact, there have been times when God was warning or encouraging you, and your flesh part simply denied it. Your flesh part thought that the message couldn't be from God; it was just a coincidence or a dream. But deep down inside your spirit part hears these messages and really knows that if the message is in line with God's Word, you can count on it. If the message you received encouraged you to break any of God's rules, then it came from somewhere else.

As you continue to feed and respect your spirit part through prayer and study, you can continue to get stronger and bolder in knowing the ways in which God speaks to you. Through faith, there are many ways of letting your spirit part receive what God wants you to hear. What is really required is willingness. Sometimes God speaks to us through a still and small voice, like He did to Elijah. We have to be willing to hear it.

Sometimes it may feel like an intuition or a "sixth sense." We have to be willing to listen to our intuitions. Sometimes God speaks to us through the things we call coincidences, if we are willing to pay attention to them.

One friend of mine prays and so strongly expects an answer that she will listen for it everywhere she goes. She might hear it through a Scripture reading, a sermon, Bible studies, other people or even on the radio. She knows that God will answer her; she simply searches until she finds it. "Seek and ye shall find, knock and it shall be opened to you." (Matthew 7:7)

Your flesh part may object to interpreting your dreams and life experiences through faith. Your flesh part might question, saying, "How do you know this? Where is the proof? This sounds like what crazy people do!" But your spirit part knows that all of the important people of faith in the Bible and elsewhere understand the events of their lives through faith.

God speaks to us in so many ways. Sometimes you just know that God is leading you to paths of righteousness. It feels right and true. God speaks to us through our dreams. Will you dare to understand them through your faith? God speaks to us through so-called coincidences. Will you dare to understand them through your spirit part? God speaks to us through music, through hymns. Will you dare to sing along and hear what is said to you? Sometimes, God even speaks to us through our pain and frustration. Will you listen with your spirit part instead of your flesh part?

Sometimes God speaks to us through our feelings. For instance, when we are really lonely, sometimes it means we have drifted away from God. Sometimes when we have been bored, it was because we weren't listening to hints of an exciting new discovery waiting for us. Your spirit part may get excited that I am talking about this, because it may want to assist you in discovering more of the ways that God is giving you encouragement. You may even feel a little bit excited now, and you can in the future as well because living by faith in the Word of God is the most exciting life. Your flesh part may object because it just doesn't know how exciting and how full of new adventures a life of faith can be. Your spirit part knows.

It is my prayer that each of us commit to walking by faith in at least one area in the next few days. I pray that in the next few days, we understand at least one event through our faith and our spirit part so that we sense God's Spirit in a powerful way. I pray especially that you sense in some way that God loves you and cares about you. Amen.

What Is Real Righteousness?
                 Jer 33: 14-16, 1 Thess 5:1-6, Lk 21: 25-36

Signs are everywhere—if you look for the right ones.

Just what is righteousness anyway? Many of us think we know what it is. In fact, we may be sure that we know. But what is it really? For many of us, our view of it is probably flawed because of what we have learned from the world. The distortion crept in when we weren't looking and we just assumed that we had the correct definition of the word. Well, maybe not.

One righteous person I know is a recovering alcoholic and drug addict. He did some bad things in his past. His image of righteousness was distorted but now he is growing. He is dependent on God for his sobriety, his humility, his truth and his genuine compassion. He is willing to learn what God wants of him. He trusts God to lead him into more righteousness. To me, this man tells the whole story. He does not necessarily fit the world's definition of a righteous person but he fits mine. He might add that he has a long way to go, but you know, I think he may just live a long life and get there.

Considering the world's view of righteousness, some of us may have been right in avoiding it! Movies, television and other forms of popular culture often portray righteous people as passive, controlled, weak, unreal, boring, rigid, self-deceiving, deprived or "tightly wound." Nothing could be farther from the truth. The great people of faith in the Bible were like some of us. They were very real. They were active, adventuresome and free. Their lives were filled with excitement, fulfillment and self-truth. The great people of faith in today's world are strong and active. They are able to do things they never thought possible before they developed a strong faith in God. People of faith are able truly to face themselves and their situations. They know they are important and of value. I know many.

The world often distorts what it means to be righteous because we are supposed to hold popular culture's view of it. There is even more distortion over how to become righteous. If asked, most people would say something like, "Just don't do bad stuff!" Evil attempts to portray the righteous person as iron-willed, able nearly to bend steel with willpower or sheer determination alone. But people who are truly righteous are supple. They find decision-making easy because they know it has little to do with willpower. It is based on a deep relationship of trust in God as our coach and leader.

Some of us have had miraculous changes in our lives when we asked God to help us. We asked him to clean up our language, change our habits or take away some urge. And he did. Many of us change more slowly, though. For many of us the road to righteousness has been slow and bumpy.

Maybe at first we looked for a miraculous change but then we simply trusted God. And we found help, sometimes in strange places. It may have come in the quiet, or from watching someone else's mistakes and learning from them. It may have come from seeing someone succeed and studying how they did it. Sometimes in the blessings of others, we get encouragement. The people who are successful are the ones who go to God first. When God helps you to let go of something, the struggle is milder.

When you know that you have been led to righteousness by God's grace, you are filled with appreciation. The next step will be exciting because you don't know where God will lead you! Yet we do know that it will be good for us. Abraham's life was one of righteousness because he had faith in God's promises. There are many, many promises in the Bible. God's promises are sure.

Of course along the journey there will be temptations. A righteous path is one where we trust God's promises more than the world's. After getting burned a few times, we realize pretty quickly that the real promises are in God's blessings. The Bible does warn us that pain and suffering will fall on the just and the unjust. We will encounter grief, sadness and pain. But with our faith, we can get through these things. We can realize later when we look back on those times that God was there for us, giving us comfort, strength and guidance. When people of faith are knocked down, they usually get up, stronger than before because they have been willing to learn from their mistakes. If you haven't been learning from your mistakes lately, take a look at how much sin is in your life. And call God immediately. He can help you to learn from your mistakes.

I can almost hear some of you saying, "Yes, but I don't feel very righteous. In fact, at times, I feel defeated, tempted, ashamed of my past and afraid about my future." Hallelujah! You are noticing how you feel. You can also notice how comforting prayer is to you as you become even more aware. Trust in God and things will begin to come to you. The path may be slow at times, but He will give you comfort. At times you may feel that your growth comes in big leaps and bounds. For all of these times, we can feel grateful that God has guided and led us. Psalm 100 says, "Enter His gates with thanksgiving and His courts with praise." This is how we get close to God. We get blessed by trusting His word and His promises.

It is my prayer that each of us feel God's presence so powerfully that we could smile inside because of the reassurance that we feel, and because of the blessings we are beginning to realize are ours. Amen.

Serenity comes when we give up false control to get real peace.

Lord, help us to bring to You our concerns, cares and worries, so that we can let go of them and relax in Your peace. We need to find Your Sabbath rest that gives us true peace. Guide us now to that place of faith inside of ourselves where we can connect with You and sense your presence here. Let us hear individually what You want us to hear.

"For to us a child is born . . ." *For* and *to* us. This is for us, this birth. God's actions and words are *for* us and *to* us. This is how we can get a great deal from the Bible, by reading it as written *for* us and *to* us. It is sacred because it is God's Word to us. The truths of the Bible are as deep as you are willing to discover. What's required is faith, a faith of openness to receive the Truth. God wants us to be open to His teaching. Over-doing skepticism closes doors. Truth is understood with a mindset of openness. We can come to the Bible with this willingness to discover its truths, remain open to its teachings, and then build other truths upon the truths we learn there.

"For to us a child is born . . ." A child changes us. A child needs and loves us. A child seems to encourage us to love. Each word of this passage of the Bible can reveal truth to us, if we have the faith of an open mind and a willingness to learn. "And his name will be called . . ." In Biblical thought, a person' s name wasn't just a label. It expressed the essential nature of the person. This is true for us as well, even though we don't think of it this way sometimes. Your name represents you. When you like yourself, you like your name. When people don't like themselves, they often do not like their names.

" . . . and his name will be called Wonderful Counselor, Mighty God, Everlasting Father, Prince of Peace." Our God's name is Wonderful Counselor. He is and will be our Counselor. A Wonderful Counselor. The Bible tells us the kings of Israel always had counselors. So I guess we are also royalty as we have a Counselor, too! And He is faithful and truthful.

The trouble is that sin causes us to deny the truth of the Bible sometimes. Sin wants us to think that we are in charge, and that we know what's truthful and what isn't. Here's the problem: Once we have picked out what we like and don't like, how do we really know what's truthful and what isn't? It wasn't a reliance on God that chose for us, it was our own egos. God never tells us to pick and choose among His truths.

Understanding the Bible with faith means accepting its truths even when we find things there that are disagreeable to us. Our sinful self says, "How dare the Bible say things that disagree with what I think and feel?" Where did any of us get such a foolish idea, that we know better than God? And yet, who among us has not acted this way, setting things aside that were not convenient or agreeable at the moment?

A more faithful approach is prayerfully to ask God to help us understand His word and His truth, and accept it in our lives. Sin causes us to hide, distort, excuse and lie. No wonder we sometimes have a hard time trusting God's Word. Sin can be a powerful thing. But through our faith, we can set these behaviors aside by asking God to help us. Titus 1: 15-16 reads, "To the pure all things are pure, but to the corrupt and unbelieving nothing is pure. Their very minds and consciences are corrupted. They profess to know God, but they deny him by their actions."

I have talked with many people who have shared with me how God has been their Wonderful Counselor. He directed them to see their mistakes and He has helped them to change. They have allowed God into their lives in ways they had not before. You may know that this is also true of you. You have been letting God's Word in, and you have been receiving it with faith. It shows when you do this. You feel different inside and other people sense the change in you.

Of course, there are other areas of our lives where we will need to listen to our Wonderful Counselor so that instead of suffering, we can change and receive His blessings. Micah 6: 8 states, " . . . what does the Lord require of you but to do justice, and to love kindness, and to walk humbly with your God?" When we walk humbly, we can hear the truth of what God is saying to us.

It is wonderful to know that we have a Counselor who will walk with us and who will help us. Serenity comes when we give up false control to get real peace. Be humble with God and ask Him to help you develop a new attitude. Maybe you have low self-esteem; you want to think more highly of yourself. You may realize that you have been putting others ahead of yourself in ways that have left you feeling badly. Your Counselor awaits you. You will find as the Living Word gets more and more fully into your spirit, you will know more of your own value and worth. Remember God's Words to you, " . . . seek ye first the kingdom of God, and his righteousness; and all these things shall be added unto you." (Matthew 6:33)

It is my prayer that each of us can come to realize more fully that God has been wanting to bless us. I pray that during difficult times, we turn to the One who can help us overcome our struggles. Amen.

The dream is true.

"Sing aloud, O daughter of Zion; shout, O Israel! Rejoice and exult with all your heart, O daughter Jerusalem!" But many people find it difficult to rejoice. They may have lost loved ones, or may be experiencing health crises or tragedies of some kind. Maybe there's an unrealized family you wanted that you do not have. Maybe during previous holiday seasons, you were let down by family members. Or perhaps you've been rejected by someone or feel left out by members of your family. Maybe you feel the pinch of financial pressure or perhaps you feel that you have let someone down. Some people even feel angry with God or disappointed by fate. These can all be difficult things, often exacerbated during holidays. It seems that the Christmas season can especially have this effect on some people. Holiday lights twinkle and other people all seem so happy.

The people to whom Zephaniah spoke were very much in the same boat. They were captives; they'd lost their very freedom, as well as their homes and contact with loved ones. They were treated like slaves with no recourse for appeal. Anything that reminded them of their former lives probably brought up very similar feelings to what some of us experience during the holidays. Many of them had given up hope of ever seeing their homes again. And isn't it hard to find hope when you've been feeling so down?

Yet God, through the prophet Zephaniah, said, "Sing aloud . . . shout . . . rejoice and exult with all your heart . . ." The passage doesn't say to do it if you want to. It says to sing, shout, rejoice and be glad. This is a little confrontational for many of us, isn't it? We believe that God is important to us, yet sometimes we sink into despair, far from a glad heart.

In a very important passage, Verse 15 gives us the reason to rejoice. It reads, "The Lord has taken away the judgments against you, he has turned away your enemies. The king of Israel, the Lord, is in your midst; you shall fear disaster no more." Who of us doesn't want the judgments against us taken away? It's the same as in Zephaniah's day. Those people desperately wanted the pain, guilt and punishment to go away. They had no date for release, and yet the Lord told them to rejoice! People who can face the pain, accept it and then rejoice anyway are to be praised. They have a deep understanding of this passage. The person who can rejoice in spite of all of their hardships has a deep wisdom that comes from God.

Lets' go on a journey to Assyria in Zephaniah's time. Imagine with me the scene in 670 BCE. Perhaps you can see the dusty streets and hear the sounds of animals. People are milling about in the tasks of everyday life . . . you hear the rustle of cloth, the slap of a sandal. You may hear people talking quietly or maybe you see people being still. You may even sense the excitement in the air. The prophet is preaching in the town square and you know that he speaks for God. Even so, you're so accustomed to hearing criticism that you are only paying partial attention to what he is saying. Nonetheless, suddenly you hear him say, "Rejoice, for God has forgiven you. He has given you a pardon. He has set aside all of your sins. He has taken away all of the judgments against you."

You can hardly believe what you are hearing. Wow! The prophet of God has just told you that you are totally free of all of the things of your past that you have done. What a wonderful blessing! You are so relieved. Something inside of you tells you that it is actually true. What you wanted so much is true. You have a new beginning.

When Zephaniah says, "rejoice," you are ready. You are ready to sing and to shout Hallelujah! You can enjoy that image as long as you like, and when you have seen all that you want and are ready to come back to the here and now, you can bring those good feelings with you. The dream is true. If you have been afraid to believe the dream, then talk to God about it. God can help you to heal from whatever difficulty you've had. If you've been afraid to let yourself be led, then talk to God about it. If you have been afraid to let yourself hope, talk to Him. If you've been afraid to feel forgiven, talk to God. He will rejoice that you are letting Him help you. He will be happy to assist you because He loves you.

We can hear the rejoicing in God's Words, too, and be glad and put them into practice in our lives. We, too, can look for how God is in our midst, and we, too, can look for how God is blessing us right now. Like those ancient people to whom Zephaniah spoke, we can search for ways of making this time a time of rejoicing. We, too, can search for the positive and then dwell on these things. This passage challenges us to dwell upon God's goodness and to rejoice and be glad. It is a responsibility but one that can bring us great rewards.

Each of us can do more of this, rather than dwelling on the negative. That's easy to do, but where does it take us? Only to despair. Let us dwell instead on our blessings and be glad. This is what Zephaniah challenges us to do: to rejoice and be glad in spite of all the rest.

This is my prayer—that we can increasingly allow God to bless us in this way. Amen.

A wish for Christmas: Lord, many of us have feelings of sadness, guilt, remorse and fear. Many of us have been trying not to feel these emotions. Some of us have put on a false face to cover what we have felt inside. Help us to let all of these emotions go and focus on You. Lead our hearts and minds to that emotional place where we can really sense Your presence. Let each of us come to feel known and cared about in a deeper way.

Once the angels had left them and gone to Heaven, the shepherds said to one another, "Let us go now to Bethlehem and see this thing that has taken place, which the Lord has made known to us." Even after the angels had left them, the shepherds continued to believe. They must have been people of deep faith not to doubt at this point. You know how it is. You have a deep and powerful spiritual experience with God. Later, it's more difficult to be so sure and positive about it.

The shepherds' deep faith prepared them for the deep experience with the angels. They were primed to let these experiences seep into their awareness. Despite the fact that there were many important, wealthy, and high-status people around Bethlehem, it was the shepherds—people of lower status and wealth— who received God's message. Because of their deep faith, the shepherds were primed: ready, hoping, expecting and open to receive the awareness of God's presence with them. God shows no partiality for our earthly hierarchies. He knows who's tuned in to receive. Many people miss being able to really sense God's presence with them because they are not tuned in; they are not open to receive. They may think that God's presence can only be felt in certain ways by certain people or under certain conditions. It is when we are open to notice how God will be with us that we can sense His presence.

Of course, we don't know all that motivated the shepherds that night. They may have been curious. Aren't we like that? We find ourselves wanting to check out and reaffirm our beliefs. Sometimes we even have felt guilty for seeking this reassurance. We wonder if this means that we do not have enough faith. God used the shepherds' desire for reassurance to bless them, though. They went and they saw and they were blessed. Mary and Joseph also sought reassurance. Reassurance is important to all of us. We all need it from time to time—even ministers and chaplains! Often in my work, I have seen the deep faith of believers and have seen how they let God heal their hurts so they could show more fruits of the Spirit. I know then that we serve a powerful God and my faith gets strengthened.

More happened that night. Mary and Joseph ended up in a place where there were no familiar faces. There were no family members present to offer them support. Mary was young and, no doubt, would have wanted the comfort of her mother as she gave birth in this strange place. For this young couple that night, not much seemed to be going their way. They were operating on faith alone. Imagine how strained that faith must have been as desperation crept in. Then the shepherds came and told them of their experience with the angels. No doubt this offered Mary and Joseph a great deal of reassurance that things were going to be all right after all. There's not much doubt in my mind that the shepherds did indeed bring this kind of reassurance to both Mary and Joseph. You know how different you feel when you sit with a person of faith. You can almost feel their sense of calm. You can sense their peace and you begin to feel it, too. Mary and Joseph needed this, they received it, and their fear and doubt lessened.

This is what we do for each other. You may have brought reassurance to some who desperately needed it. You may have been a mother and father figure for someone, reassuring a young person who was confused, frightened or lonely. Or you may have been a son or daughter figure for someone. You may have brought reassurance to parents who lost children or who experienced a break with a child. You may represent to someone a caring aunt or uncle, a sister and a brother. In healing our hurts from the past, we all need each other. At times we represent family members who cannot or will not show the compassion, care and forgiveness that we need. Thank God that we can receive these things from Him through others who care for us and are with us.

Verse 19 says, " . . . Mary treasured all these words and pondered them in her heart." To ponder means to dwell upon deeply. Mary kept those things that were told to her that night and she dwelled upon them. I keep as special the notes and cards of people who have let me know that God has touched their lives. I dwell on those comments; some sustain and build my faith. Like you, I like to remember these special things. What we dwell on inside of ourselves changes us. When we dwell on those times in our lives when God was clearly present, it brings back that sense of reassurance and peace. When you dwell on those times, you remember that God was blessing you and protecting you—sometimes in spite of yourself! You can be blessed again as you feel His reassurance and presence all over again. You remember God's grace and mercy, and you know you are loved.

It is my prayer at Christmas that we all are able to sense a portion of how much we are loved, and offer reassurance and compassion to others. Amen.

Having a "hope" mindset is completely different from having a mindset of defeat. Both will bring about what we expected.

Many of us have experienced disappointment in life when our expectations were not fulfilled. In fact, I bet everyone has. When you expect something in your life—a phone call, a letter, a promotion or something else—and it doesn't happen, you can feel sorely disappointed. Or you ask for something in prayer, something that is very important to you, and it does not seem to happen in the way that you asked. We can get very hurt and angry when this happens. Perhaps, though, the fault lies in the narrowness of our expectations.

I knew a young man once who grew up in a family where his parents did not get along. From the time he was seven or eight, he prayed that his parents would stay together so that he could belong to an intact family. His parents continued to fight, though, and eventually, they divorced. After a time, both married other people. The boy was crushed. He had expected that God would answer his heartfelt prayer. He thought that he'd been taught that if you asked God for good things, God would give them to you. He found himself angry with God and losing faith in the whole idea of religion. The young man started getting into trouble. His conflict with his mother increased and he began staying away from home a lot. Eventually, one of his friend's families took him in. These people treated him with respect. They praised his efforts and trusted him with responsibility. This family was not without conflict, but through counseling and through their faith, the parents had stayed together and had improved their relationship.

One day it dawned on the young man that God *had* answered his prayers. He was now part of a family with an intact set of parents. He felt that he had a place to belong. As he healed and felt better about himself, he was able to reach out to his own mother. He had been as angry with her as he was at God. He loved his mother deeply, but he had been afraid to reach out to her for fear of being hurt and disappointed. As he realized that his prayers had been answered, he was able to reach out to God again. He realized the narrowness of his expectations had set him up for disappointment.

In Micah's day, Israel was under siege and had little hope of prevailing against the invaders. Most of Israel had already been conquered; just a tiny remnant stood against the invaders. Things were very bleak, indeed. Many people believed that as the captive nation's citizens were assimilated into the conquerors' culture, Israel would cease to exist as a distinct nation. This would mean giving up not only their way of life but also their religion. The invaders believed in a different god and would force their beliefs upon the Israelites. Many, many people had lost all hope. Not Micah, though. He predicted that Israel would survive and that a mighty leader would come from Bethlehem. Many did not believe this but Micah did. He hoped for and believed in what God had told him.

During my career, I have seen many people hold on to hope against the odds. Many times, blessings have come, though often in ways they did not expect. I have seen imprisoned women who had no hope of release hold on to hope of receiving God's blessings. I've seen people reconciled with family members when there was no earthly reason to believe it would ever happen. There have been miracles of restoration among family members, miracles of re-established contact, miracles of continued support, of deepened relationships. Many of these people were open to discovering what God's blessings might look like.

In the course of a day, if things are not going the way that you planned or expected, the world is apt to say that you are having a bad day. The world's view might tell you are unlucky. You know the kind of things people say: "Why, he wouldn't have any luck at all if it weren't for bad luck." You may even have said these kinds of things about yourself. "That's the way things always seem to go for me. That's just my luck. I don't want to get my hopes up because things never go right for me."

Where in the Bible were we ever taught to talk like that? All of those negative predictions, the doom and gloom, come from the earthly realm. They do not come from God. We are told that our dreams, hopes, expectations and even our words are important. The Bible says in Psalm 118:24, "This is the day that the Lord has made; let us rejoice and be glad in it." Even on those days when things do not seem to be going the way that we want, we can look for God's blessings. In fact, these are the days when we most need to look for them. It's when we seek that we find.

This passage in Micah challenges us to look at our days through God's expectation, not the world's narrow view. When we find that things do not seem to be going our way, we can search for God's blessings. We can expect God's blessings even when we are finding other ways that God is blessing us. He wants to bless us. He wants us to hold on to our faith, to remain hopeful and to expect miracles. I challenge you to catch yourself if you say negative things—gibberish—about bad luck or some negative expectation. Instead, look for God's blessings in an open way. Give God enough room for you to be able to see the blessings He has and is preparing for you.

My prayer is that each of us can recognize that we are loved, this day and every day. Amen.

Giving Control Back To The Shepherd
                                 Lk 2: 1-14

No ordinary shepherd . . .

A decree went out from the Roman emperor Augustus, the most powerful man in the ancient world, a man who could decide who lived and who died. It is ironic that through his decree that all be registered, Caesar Augustus did God's bidding. His decree helped bring about the historical event that had been prophesied hundreds of years earlier. Jesus was supposed to be born in Bethlehem, in the city where David was born. Because of Augustus' decree, Mary and Joseph went to Bethlehem and the prophecy was fulfilled. It is interesting how God works sometimes, isn't it? It seems that earthly things like politics are in charge of our lives, yet if we look deeper, we can see often that God has made changes that bring more of His grace and love into our lives.

The name Bethlehem has special meaning. It means "house of bread." Perhaps it is no accident that bread was so important in Jesus' ministry. When we receive communion, or recall the miracle of the loaves and fishes, bread is important. Jesus ultimately referred to himself as bread. Often, the most common everyday things—like bread—can make the biggest impact on us spiritually. "Give us this day our daily bread, " says the Lord's Prayer.

Jesus was born in the "house of bread"—Bethlehem. There was no place for him at the inn, and he was born in a manger in a stable. In those days, people did not have babies in hospitals. They had them at home, perhaps attended by a midwife. Poor people had babies wherever they could and often, under difficult circumstances. In today's terms, the situation of Jesus' birth would be like a child being born in a parking garage, and then laid in a cardboard box in the back of a pickup truck.

I wonder how the innkeeper felt who turned away this couple and this child being born. Years later, when he realized he had turned away the Messiah, the Lord of Lords, the Prince of Peace, how did he feel? Yet what if the innkeeper had registered Mary and Joseph? Herod would have found Jesus, and the innkeeper might have been persecuted. Maybe God was looking out for this man. I wonder if the innkeeper was changed later in life when he realized what had really happened in his stable. After all, we are all changed when we get closer to God. As people sense the genuineness of your heart, they are also urged to change. People can sense whether you love God or not. They can sense when God's Spirit is present. God is always inviting and encouraging us—never demanding—that we accept Him

Some people are notified directly from Heaven. Perhaps they are more tuned in to spiritual matters. The wise men were seeking Jesus by following the Star of his birth and the prophecies. Because he was faithful and followed God's law, the man named Simeon was blessed when he saw the baby Jesus. The shepherds were notified of Jesus' birth by an angel.

The image of the shepherd is all through the Bible. The Messiah was to be a shepherd to his people. As Psalm 23 says, "The Lord is my shepherd . . ." Ezekiel tells us that the Messiah would be like a shepherd to his people. The night of Jesus' birth, an angel approached the shepherds. Why these shepherds? God has purpose and intention in His selection. Those the Lord chooses might not be the world's popular choices. When the Lord accepts us as one of His sheep, it's because He saw something in us. He is encouraging us toward Him. He chooses us because we have faith and that faith is reflected in our actions. He might even see this before we do!

Jews know Deuteronomy 6:4 very well. "Hear, O Israel, the Lord is our God, the Lord alone. You shall love the Lord your God with all your heart, and with all your soul, and with all your might." The verse continues with, "Keep these words that I am commanding you today in your heart. Recite them to your children and talk about them when you are home and when you are away, when you lie down and when you rise."

We are to keep God's commandments in our hearts and minds, and on our lips continuously. Paul told us to pray without ceasing, to be continuously thankful and in communication with God. When we allow the Lord's Words to dwell in our hearts and minds, it changes us. Romans 12: 2 says " . . . be transformed by the renewing of your minds. . . ." This renewal comes from God. Sometimes it can feel frightening. If we've been living with shame for many years, it might feel odd to begin to leave that shame behind. If others have mistreated us, it may not be easy at first to trust God.

We're not the only ones afraid. The shepherds were but the angels told them not to be. When angels first encounter someone, they often have to tell them to relax. Fear of the awesomeness of God is pretty common. Joseph was afraid when the angels notified him. The disciples were afraid when the risen Lord met them. Yet being blessed is something that God does want for us. "Glory to God in the highest heaven and on earth peace among those whom he favors!"

It is my prayer that we allow the awesomeness of God's love in. He was born in human form to be here with us, and to love and teach us. I pray that we acknowledge who is really in charge of the world, and who it is who has the final say about what is and is not important. Amen.

There are clues for which you can watch.

As the shepherds, wise men and other people visiting the baby Jesus left, God gave Mary and Joseph a sign. Joseph saw in a dream that Herod wanted to harm Jesus. Working through Herod, evil was trying to attack Jesus at a most vulnerable time, when he was a baby. Evil did not then and does not now want Jesus to succeed. Jesus represents goodness, honesty, truth and God's desire for all of us to receive grace and blessings, and evil's power was and is threatened by truth and grace.

Throughout Jesus' ministry, there were many people who did not like him. They even hated him for what he represented. Jesus told us that we could expect the same treatment. It is true that some people will be inspired when they see Christ in you, but some will be angry with you. It might be because you are succeeding and doing things right. It might be because you stand for truth. It might be because you look and feel better and this is threatening to them because they are not heading in that direction. Sin and the fruit of the flesh produce hatred, envy and strife. These things might be directed at you as you change in positive ways. But Jesus tells us to count this as joy, thankful that our faith is having such a big impact.

Of course, this is easier said than done! When people dislike us, our first reaction is to examine ourselves. "What have I ever done to that person?" we ask. This is okay because this self-assessment keeps us honest. But some people are going to dislike us even when we've done nothing against them. They are in a struggle with themselves. They might dislike us because we remind them of someone from their past with whom they did not get along. This antagonistic behavior might be more pronounced in January, as many folks who have held it together during the holidays—a time of hurt, disappointment and self-punishment for them— begin to feel irritable and cranky. Did you know that in prisons there are more arguments, fights, and people locked down in January than in any other month?

There are clues you can watch for, though, to keep yourself safer. People who are about to explode in anger will show signs of increasing irritability as the situation escalates. You can walk away. That is what Mary and Joseph did after God warned Joseph in the dream to protect Mary and Jesus. There are a lot of other ways to cope when others are angry with us. We can explore with them rationally reasons for the conflict. Some situations can be resolved. Some folks, though, are going to be angry with us anyway. It just might be because of your faith. They're probably not going to say, "I don't like her because she has changed her life. She is no longer in trouble and she has the Spirit of God in her." They may try to discredit you. They many call you a hypocrite. Yet remember that we can count it as joy. We can be thankful that our faith has a big impact. We can also pray for guidance.

Ideally, in difficult situations, we want to continue to reflect Jesus and not a "fleshly" attitude of getting even. After warning us to be as wise as serpents, Jesus told us to be as gentle as doves. Matthew 10: 24-26 says, "A disciple is not above the teacher, not a slave above the master; it is enough for the disciple to be like the teacher, and the slave like the master. . . . So have no fear of them; for nothing is covered up that will not be uncovered, and nothing secret that will not become known."

Joseph received signs from God. They were signs to leave Israel and to return at the appropriate time. As people of faith, we receive many, many signs from God. Some are as dramatic as the ones Joseph received. Some are subtler. God often gives us signs yet we do not always pay attention to them. As we become more honest, though, by our faith and by reading God's Word, our intuition improves. Sometimes the sign may be an odd feeling, that something is drawing you toward it or warning you away from something. Sometimes you might feel drawn to a particular passage in the Bible. Maybe a sign will come in your dreams. The Holy Spirit speaks to us in diverse ways.

Ignoring the call of God can also lead to certain feelings. I know one woman who ignored the signs that her husband was molesting her children. She began to get depressed. The more she ignored her intuitions, the more depressed she became. I know another woman who ignored the way her husband and her family used and exploited her. She became anxious and thought that it was all her fault. She wanted a pill to take away the anxiety. I know people who have ignored their own responsibility and their own need for forgiveness. They hid these feelings in depression. I know people who hide their guilt through anger or their sin through fear. We've all ignored our true intuitions. We all know only too well the price we pay when we do so.

But how do you know if a sign is from God? If it produces the fruits of the Spirit—peace, kindness, gentleness, joy, love and self-control—it is from God. The fruits of the flesh are envy, bitterness, hatred, jealousy and the flaunting of sin. One of the best things is that the more we look for God's signs, the more we will see them and the more affirmation we'll receive.

It is my prayer that each us will notice the signs that God is giving us now. And I pray that we will be aware of how much He loves us and cares about us. Amen.

Do not be conformed to this world . . .

"In the beginning was the Word, and the Word was with God, and the Word was God." This has a familiar ring to it. The first words of Genesis, of course, are "In the beginning . . ." We know right away that what we are about to hear is foundational to the message. John echoes this, and begins his Gospel with, "In the beginning was the Word." In the beginning God created the heavens and the earth by speaking them into existence. It's a powerful image that God made something happen by speaking words.

Scientists now are exploring what the faithful have known for a long time, that prayer and God's Words make us feel better. It's one of the reasons we go to church. When we read and hear God's Words and meditate on their meaning we feel better and we change. It's like being exposed to the sun. It feels good and it changes our skin. When we are exposed to God's Words, we feel better and it changes our spirits. Often we can feel the peace of God when we read His Word. We can sense the calm and see the difference in how we see things. Evil often tries to steal this from us by exposing us to the ugliness of sin. Sometimes we have let evil steal our blessings when we have dwelled on the ugliness of a sinful attitude. Instead, we can dwell on God's Word and return to that sense of peace inside ourselves. Thoughts are converted in our brains into biochemical reactions. These reactions change us on a molecular level. When you open yourself up to God's Word through faith, you are opened up to God's healing power and to life.

A paradox of faith and acceptance is clearly seen in cases of serious illness. When people who are ill let themselves trust God's goodness and His plan for their lives, even if it means the end, they are more likely to recover. People who are unwilling to search for God's blessings even in their illnesses almost never have spontaneous healing. People who make peace with their conditions and accept their bodies, situations and options, looking for God's blessings, do better.

One way to look at disease is as an attempt to get us to do what is better for us. The diabetic who accepts the diet limitations the illness requires will live longer and be healthier. I know a man whose family has a history of gall bladder problems. He knew that eating foods with a high fat content would be painful for him and figured that his illness was God's way of getting him to eat a healthier diet. The reality is that we heal in some way when we accept our powerlessness over our condition. For one thing, we pray sooner when we face our powerlessness. Did you know that recent studies that have shown that people who are prayed for, whether they know it or not, heal quicker and more completely, with fewer complications? God has given us prayer. It's our way to connect with Him.

God tells us that the spoken word is important. So we need to be mindful of the Word of God as expressed in James 3:10. "From the same mouth come blessings and cursing. My brothers and sisters, this ought not to be so." James 3:6 reads, "And the tongue is a fire. The tongue is placed among our members as a world of iniquity; it stains the whole body, sets on fire the cycle of nature, and is itself set on fire by hell." In other words, we are to watch what we say. Much of the time, we use our words to try to increase our sense of power. But this is dangerous. Jesus said it this way in Matthew 5:37: "Let your word be 'Yes, Yes' or 'No, No'; anything more than this comes from the evil one." For example, when someone swears on their family member's grave or life, it probably means that they are being dishonest.

One of the most difficult things for people to accept is that when they pray, something bad may still happen. Here, we need to keep a harness on what we think. First, God works in mysterious ways. And what we say and do is a later result of what we thought. Rom 12: 2 says, "Do not be conformed to this world, but be transformed by the renewing of your minds, so that you may discern what is the will of God - what is good and acceptable and perfect." The more we think God's thoughts by reading His Word and getting it into our hearts, minds and spirits, the more it becomes a part of our very being. It urges us toward the Light, health, blessings, and toward God's will for us.

None of us is ever going to be able to control completely what is on our minds or what comes out of our mouths. We could all do a much better job. We can remember that we don't want foul things coming from the same mouths that praise God. I know many people who have changed their language. I know many people who have changed their thoughts and behaviors through faith. Jesus said that as people think in their hearts, they are. Those thoughts are words. When we put God's Words there, they have a positive effect.

If God has touched you, He has done so through His Words. If your life is truly changed, then the light of His Word has been guiding you and is in you. "In the beginning was the Word." When you study, read or hear the Word, meditate on it. Listen to sermons. Dwell on a passage or verse. Then you are taking God's Word inside of you.

It is my prayer that we allow the Holy Spirit to guide, lead and direct our hearts and minds as we study God's Word. I pray we will be of one mind and one accord with the Lord. Amen.

You Can Receive God's Grace In Your Life
Mt 3: 13-17, Acts 10: 34-43, Isa 42: 1-7

It's often when we are willing to admit our inability that God gives us the ability.

Jesus went to John for a public baptism. There's a lot of symbolism in this first verse. Jesus went to Galilee, known as a sinful place, and to the Jordan River. The Jordan was the symbol of crossing over into God's Promised Land. It conveys God's blessing and the idea of going through life with God's guidance. Jesus went to these places intentionally and with humility. It's important to note that this is where Jesus began his ministry - from a position of humility. All ministries, including witnessing, are best done through humility. All living is best done with humility. John's humility showed when he objected to Jesus' proposal. He knew what it meant to baptize the Christ. Well aware of his own sins, he did not feel worthy.

So John saw his own sins. The righteous always do. Paul described himself as the worst sinner. So did Mother Theresa. To be truly righteous, we need to realize our own sinfulness and unworthiness. How better to know God's grace? Real righteousness depends on God's Word, not on human achievement or skills or capabilities or boastfulness. When God declares us to be clean, we are aware that we have been forgiven and accepted.

When Jesus was clear with John about wanting to be baptized, John did comply. Jesus said, "Let it be so now; for it is proper for us in this way to fulfill all righteousness." Being righteous means for us to put into action God's Word and will in our lives. It means living under the authority of Scripture and of the law.

I used to tell inmates at the prison that even though the parole board, the criminal justice system, our government, and every authority figure we know do things that sometimes seem foolish, dumb, unjust or just plain wrong, if we really believe that God is in charge—if we really believe that "all things work together for the good of those who love and serve the Lord"—that even though something might look dumb, we know that God is going to use it for His work. There may be evil working, too, but people who are helped by evil do not see how evil will turn on them and how much they will pay in the long run.

So Jesus and John submitted to what they knew was required. They were humble and allowed God to be their director. Righteousness requires this kind of cooperation with God. Being humble is the greatest gift you can give yourself because it means that you can find your way to the ultimate in truth, love and forgiveness. We all have a need for God's grace. It's not just the lowest of us but the highest as well. Righteousness knows that we all have the same need for cleansing and grace. Sin is arrogant, rude and proud. Righteousness is humble, has manners, treats others as equals—or better—and is meek.

In our Christian tradition, baptism connotes acceptance into the family of God. If you haven't been baptized before, you may choose to be. But what do we do after we've been baptized and we backslide? The answer is: Pray! We can reach out to God with prayer. True, some may want to be baptized again. Others may want to make a public repentance. Others may need to confess and repent with one other person. The Bible does tell us to confess our sins to one another. But if baptism were the only way for us to grow spiritually, we all might as well get used to staying wet! We can't achieve righteousness through baptism. Baptism is our entrance into the family of God, not an eraser for all of our sins. The person who is baptized and does not repent is just a wet sinner!

As members of the family of God, we are to go by God's rules. The rules are to confess, repent and receive forgiveness through communion. This is why Jesus gave us the bread and the wine. We become righteous when we adopt an attitude of servitude to God and a willingness to do what He wants of us.

A real test of our righteousness can arise when we are tempted. It's in those everyday decisions we make. Will I do this or that? Will I say 'yes' or 'no'? If you're struggling, ask God for help in that area. If you don't know the areas in which you are struggling, ask God to open your eyes. Real righteousness is evident when we tell the truth, the whole truth, even when it does not make us look good. The people who are successful in stopping their lying usually must go through a period of reconciliation. They go to the people to whom they have lied and make it right. I know a man who spent three to four months tracking down the people to whom he had lied over the years and that he had hurt. He apologized to everyone he could and made right what he could. The Lord became powerful in him because he was truly repentant.

If you honestly want to put some sin behind you, pray for God's help and then confess the sin to one other person. Ask others to pray for you. God will deliver you, even when you tell yourself that what you are struggling with is unimportant. If these things are so unimportant, why do they keep coming to mind?

It is my prayer that we will be able to rejoice as we examine our lives. I pray that each of us can hear God saying, "This is my beloved in whom I am well pleased." Amen.

All things hidden shall come to light.

In this passage, God lifts up the faithful who have started to feel disheartened, useless and defeated. This describes all of us from time to time, so let us find words of encouragement and hope here.

God declared, " . . . You are my servant, Israel, in whom I will be glorified." God wants to bless us so that His love will live inside of us. He wants us to feel whole and to prosper so that others will be encouraged by what they see in us. He wants us to be righteous so we can offer grace, hope and redemption to others through the fruit we bear. God needs us and has jobs for us. This is what God told Israel yet she was demoralized. She thought she was not worthy, that her efforts had been in vain. Aware of her failures and focused on her sins, she was feeling useless and down It is true, isn't it, that when we first feel that God cares for us, we get enthused and excited and hopeful? Then life sets in, one thing after another happens, and pretty soon we don't even know how we got to despair, we just know we got there. It's easy to feel the way Israel felt.

For a wide variety of reasons, none of us has developed according to the perfected plan of God. None of us has taken that ideal path that was designed for us at the beginning. The good news is that like all winners, God has a backup plan for every one of us! If we did not fulfill His first plan, He has another for each of us. It is one that can bring blessings and one that will include all of your background, even the things that have caused you shame.

I'd like to share a story with you. One weekend, at the local trauma hospital in Louisville, Kentucky, a young woman was admitted after she attempted suicide. She had been found alive and was all right physically, but she was very emotionally distraught. She believed that she had committed an unforgivable sin and that her life was over. (Isn't it amazing that evil always wants us to think that our sin, no matter what it is, is the worst and most unforgivable?) You see, she had had an abortion and for her, that seemed like a ruinous and sinful thing. She thought she was condemned to never feel clean and good again.

That night the staff at the hospital contacted the chaplain on call, who had switched shifts with one of the other chaplains. There was no way that anyone would have known that this woman had also had an abortion and was also struggling with her feelings about it. None of her colleagues knew because she had never discussed it with anyone. She had kept it all locked away. Now, this chaplain knew in her mind that God forgave her for whatever sin there was but in her heart she had not accepted her difficult decision or forgiven herself. She had carried shame about the abortion for some time.

At first this chaplain was overwhelmed by the task in front of her. How could she talk to this depressed young woman about what was wrong when she was not even sure that her faith was supporting her? Yet she reached out. She ended up sharing with the young woman the story of her own abortion, and, in so doing, the chaplain gave her a very, very important gift - the gift of hope. The young woman began to think that maybe she could accept her decision. The chaplain received blessings that night too, because she began to feel clean and forgiven. She began to talk more about her experience with the young woman, including in her story her previous secret and shame.

Neither of these women knew in advance that they could be helpful to each other, but God blessed both of them. The Scripture reads," For I am honored in the eyes of the Lord and my God has become my strength." Both of the women let God become more of their strength that weekend. They were able to have faith that God could use something for good that they had thought was unforgivable. You see, God wanted to heal both of these women. And He did.

There is a simple truth here. We somehow think that our shame or sin is the worst even though others will not think that. The more faithful and righteous we are, the more we tend to think that our sin is the worst. The more harshly we judge others, the less room we have for faith. We can condemn sin by disliking it in ourselves but have less judgment of others. This is the way of the righteous, aware that we are less than God and that forgiveness is His gift, given when we seek it with the humility that recognizes our own sin. It is a gift to the humble.

Next God tells Israel that He is increasing her mission. She is going to be more than a servant who lifts others up, who helps restore people who have wandered off from the family. That isn't enough. God is going to send Israel (the faithful) to be a light to other nations (the non-believers). She is to reach out to all. She who was demoralized got a promotion, an even bigger job! This is what God wants: to promote us, lift us up, bless us and see us proper. He wants to give us good gifts. Of course, God may chastise you; He chastises all whom He loves because He knows that they can do better. You don't always have to know how it all works. Have faith that God can use you and begin searching for ways in which you can do something for Him.

It is my prayer that we let ourselves be open to ways in which God wants to lead us and direct our paths. Amen.

On them light has shined . . .

This passage is about distress. Can we acknowledge that we have all been in anguish? Can we also admit that our sin caught us up in the types of lifestyles and thinking that has imprisoned us? Sin tricked us and led us into things that promised fun, excitement and whatever else we thought we wanted. In reality, it delivered a hell of anguish, torment, trouble and distress. Sin stole our self-esteem, our relationships with others and God, and even our freedom. Most of us know all about anguish. This passage begins, "There will be no gloom for those who were in anguish." It's predicting your future!

The passage reads. " . . . There will be no gloom. . . ." What is the gloom from which we are being delivered? In the King James Version of the Bible, the word is translated as "dimness" or "a lack of light." This seems to connote sadness, dreariness and the heavy remorse that oppresses us when we know that we have been forgiven but when we have not yet forgiven ourselves. Could you guess that this is the attitude that sin loves to exploit? Yet God will ultimately deliver us from doom and gloom and the chronic sadness that sin exploits. It's in Scripture. There are plenty of things in the world that we can find to give us bad feelings. Philippians 4: 8 tells us, though, "Finally, beloved, whatever is true, whatever is honorable, whatever is just, whatever is pure, whatever is pleasing, whatever is commendable, if there is any excellence and if there is anything worthy of praise, think about these things."

Isn't this great? God is giving us help and delivering us from doom and gloom thinking! Earlier in Philippians, we're told, "Have no fear about anything, but in everything by prayer and supplication with thanksgiving, let your requests be known to God." That sounds pretty good, doesn't it? What happens when we pray about everything with thanksgiving and put it in His hands? We find ourselves with a thankful attitude. Verse 7 leads us to the peace of God, a peace that passes all understanding.

I realize that for some of us who have really struggled with sadness, this sounds too good to be true, a bit Polly Anna-ish even. Let's recognize that the feeling of sadness is a real emotion and not a sin. Let's recognize that many of us have lived through some very difficult times and that sadness is a natural byproduct. Thoughts from our past may intrude into our thoughts today. The thoughts of anguish, shame, remorse or embarrassment may even have surfaced in the last few moments. Well, OK. Let the doom and gloom stuff get baptized, immersed in our feelings of acceptance and thankfulness, which come when we dwell on that which is true, honorable, just, pure, lovely, gracious or excellent. God said that He is delivering us from the type of thinking that sin perpetuates by stealing our joys and blessings.

Erasing, transforming and overcoming gloom doesn't happen overnight. Yet it happens most quickly when we dwell on those things toward which God directs us. As Christians in our culture, we have not been instructed from early childhood what to dwell on in order to have such blessings. Sometimes, though, we felt rewarded for thinking the worst. It kept us safe and helped to numb the pain of disappointment.

Yet God intended for us to be blessed, encouraged, and given instruction that would keep us safe—and He tells us how. In Deuteronomy 6:6-7, we're told, "Keep these words that I am commanding you today in your heart. Recite them to your children and talk about them when you are at home and when you are away, when you lie down and when you rise." By keeping God's Word on our minds and tongues and in our hearts, we are protected. Jesus used Scripture to protect him when he was tempted. God told us to do it, too, and it works!

God sent this message to the ones in anguish," . . . the people who walked in darkness. . . ." It is the people who have lived in the darkness of sin who can see the light the best. It's easier to see a candle when there is much darkness. We don't notice it as much in the daylight. Those of us who recognize that we came from the pitch-blackness of emptiness and sin rejoice because we have seen a great light! This is for those who have lived in darkness. We have God who helps us and lifts us up. That is love!

Verse 2 concludes, "On them light has shined." It was not our effort. It was not because we deserved it or could make it happen. God has given and still gives His light to us. He wants us to be blessed and healed, and to then take His message to others. Do you remember Jesus' words in Matthew 11:29-30? They say, "Take my yoke upon you and learn from me; for I am gentle and humble in heart, and you shall find rest for your souls. For my yoke is easy and my burden is light." What a great burden to carry: Light! When we notice evil attempting to trick us with doom and gloom thinking, we can switch to light. We can switch to God's Words, to dwelling on things that are true, honorable, just, pure, lovely or gracious. We can go intentionally toward things that are excellent in God's eyes. As we do, the gloom lifts and the fear disappears or becomes transformed by the renewal of our minds.

It is my prayer that each of us will begin to discover what is good or excellent in those God created, especially in ourselves and in each other. It is right for us to give thanks for all of the blessings God has given to us. Amen.

Today's humility helps to counteract yesterday's prideful acts.

"Seek the Lord, all you humble of the land . . ." This is an invitation to the humble; the arrogant, proud and haughty are excluded. If you are humble, God likes you and wants you! His own humility respects us and blesses us, while helping to keep us safe.

So just how do we know if we are being humble? What does being humble mean? Jesus told us in the way that He respected God's Word and in the Sermon on the Mount. In Matthew 5:3, Jesus taught, "Blessed are the poor in spirit for theirs is the kingdom of heaven." He further described humility when he spoke of the meek and of those who mourn, who hunger and thirst for righteousness, who are merciful and pure in heart, who are the peacemakers and the persecuted. He described it when he spoke of those people who are reviled and persecuted, and against whom evil is uttered because of their commitment to the Lord. If you are any of these, then you are humble and Jesus is talking to you. You can rejoice and be glad! If you are not any of these things, then you may want to repent so that you also can rejoice.

Finding humility is not always easy in our world, where much of the time the humble person is not rewarded with the world's recognitions. In fact, the world tries to make the humble proud in a way that excludes God. But humility is not a degrading position. Humility is not self-disrespect. It is our proper and real self. It's who we were made to be. Jesus was humble and courageous. He demonstrated for us how humility directs our relationship toward God by showing us how employable we are in God's eyes. Moses was said to be the humblest of men. His humility was the reason that God could work through him.

Throughout the Bible, humility is described as being a state of mind and spirit where a person can be useful and blessed. Proverbs 29:23 reads, "A person's pride will bring humiliation, but one who is lowly in spirit will obtain honor." In the Book of Job it says that God saves the humble. The humble are praised in Genesis, Exodus, Deuteronomy, Judges, 2 Chronicles, Psalms, Proverbs, Isaiah, Jeremiah, Matthew, 2 Corinthians, 1 Peter and in the Book of James, where it says, "Humble yourselves before the Lord, and he will exalt you." (James 4:10)

The best test for assessing our humility is in Zephaniah 2:3, which reads, "Seek the Lord, all you humble of the land, who do his commands." The humble seek to do what God commands. If your goal is to eliminate sin from your life, if you are striving to overcome temptation, if you want to

111

follow what God tells you to do—even if you have not yet been able to do it—then you are included, encouraged, cared about and loved.

What are the outward signs of humility? People with real self-respect have no need to be arrogant or rude, no need to cut in line in front of others who are waiting, no need to put on airs, and no need to put others down. People with real self-respect know God loves them, warts and all. They are peaceful in this knowledge. They are humble and respectful toward others. Most of us are honest enough to admit that, at times, we have been disrespectful of others. Think back to one of those times. Were you acting proud because you were feeling badly about yourself? We can only respect others when we respect ourselves.

Zephaniah 3: 11 reads "On that day you shall not be put to shame because of the deeds by which you have rebelled against me . . ." In other words, our humility and our desire to do God's will by treating others as we would have them treat us are insurance against being put to shame by God for our rebellious acts. Today's humility helps to counteract yesterday's prideful sin. All sin has an element of pride in it and is hated by God. If in your past, you lied to avoid the consequences of your actions, possessing humility today will go a long way toward erasing those old lies.

Humility is a state of relationship with the Lord. It is about trusting God to help us to be honest, humble or trustworthy. We do not get to these things by ourselves. Humility is our willingness to follow the Commandments, to mourn and regret our sin, and to repent. Humility admits the truth.

Zephaniah 3:12 says, "For I will leave in the midst of you a people humble and lowly. They shall seek refuge in the name of the Lord." Why? Why would God put us with other humble people? He does this so the humble can lead the proud to the Lord. God wants to help us through each other. By imitating the people who are doing God's will, we can find the way to self-esteem and blessings. God puts humble folks in our midst who do no wrong, tell no lies, are honest and aboveboard, and who can inspire us to live better. Humble folks who are able to overcome temptation may be placed in our midst to give us hope and to show it can be done. Isn't it amazing how impossible we think it is to break some addiction or pattern of sin until we see someone else get it straight?

It is my prayer that each of us becomes willing to be led into paths of righteousness as well as made to lie down in green pastures beside still waters. I pray we will feel safe and protected, even at a table prepared for us in the presence of our enemies. I pray that we can say with the psalmist, "Surely goodness and mercy shall follow me all the days of my life, and I shall dwell in the house of the Lord forever." Amen.

Let Your Light Shine
                 Isa 58:7-10, Mt 5: 13-16, 1 Cor 2:1-5

What are your words sprinkled with?

Have you ever felt that your prayers were not being heard? Have you wondered what the problem was? This passage may give you the answer.

"Is it not to share your bread with the hungry and bring the homeless into your house . . . ?" This question refers to something mentioned earlier in the text, and asks, in effect, "What is a real fast?" In ancient times, people fasted a lot, feeling that it would somehow get God's attention focused on what they were asking of Him. With this passage, we're told clearly that a true fast involves sharing our bread with the hungry and sharing our home with the homeless. We are told to do for others who are suffering and thus put our faith into practical action. If we're around people who have food and shelter, are we off the hook? No, of course we still have responsibility *and* we have opportunity (more on that in a bit).

When we're told to feed, clothe and shelter others, we're asked literally to do these things. We're also to do them in a figurative sense. For example, there are people who hunger for genuine friendship. They want to be able to trust someone after being exploited by people in their past. Wouldn't it be nice for that individual to have a real friend who would not try to exploit him or her? There are people who are hungry to be accepted and to have respect accorded them. Wouldn't it be nice to give someone like this a compliment? Acknowledgement is something we all need on a daily basis. There are people who get ignored, shunned, and excluded from cliques or other groups. They need a home. There are people who feel desperately naked, exposed, shamed, and made fun of. They want to be clothed in acceptance, forgiveness and respect.

Sharing our bread, clothing and home is about so much more than feeding, dressing and covering with a roof. As human beings, we do have those basic needs. We also have other very important needs, though. We need acknowledgement and recognition, acceptance and nurturing. In fact, most of us can admit that in our attempts to get these things in the past, we did some pretty dumb things. We wanted acceptance and a sense of being included somewhere. You can rest assured that God knows all about these needs and, in knowing them, will be there for us.

Verse 8 says, "Then let your light break forth like the dawn, and your healing shall spring up speedily, your righteousness shall go before you, the glory of the Lord shall be your rear guard." In other words, when you reach out to others and help them, your light shall shine and your faith will be clear to others. A real way to show our loyalty to God, we're told, is by the little, everyday things that we do for others. It's nice when you're recognized, when someone wishes you a nice day, smiles at you, or remembers your name. So maybe you can do these things for others, knowing what they mean to you. It's even nicer to know that someone is praying for you, your healing, your success and your continued health.

Verse 9 reads, "Then you shall call, and the Lord will answer; you shall cry for help, and he will say, Here I am." This is a nice thought, that when we call out, God will be there for us. The bonus is that we are more aware of God listening to us when—and only when - we are willing to see the pain and the needs of others. This is what our Lord wants, for us to reach out to others and show care and compassion. Throughout the Bible, we're told over and over to let our light shine. We're told that we are the salt of the earth. We're told to take care of the fatherless, to give to the poor, to feed the hungry and to protect the weak. God wants us to reach out to others, and show care and compassion. God can't reward us, though, when we don't shine our light of love. This is from 1 John 2:9-10: "Whoever says, 'I am in the light,' while hating a brother or sister is still in the darkness. Whoever loves a brother or sister lives in the light, and in such a person there is no cause for stumbling."

Would you like your prayers to be heard? Do you want to be protected? Do you want to feel close to God? Are you willing to begin putting God's Word into practice? Do you want your righteousness to be seen by God? Then do for others. This is the way of our Lord. Put your faith into daily practice and speak to people. Be welcoming and kind. Wouldn't it be nice for your gloom to lift and for you to feel better?

Verse 9 and10 tell us how to do all of this: "If you remove the yoke from among you, the pointing of the finger, the speaking of evil, if you offer your food to the hungry and satisfy the needs of the afflicted, then your light shall rise in the darkness and your gloom be like the noonday . . ." You can begin right now: Commit to cleaning up your words and stopping your criticism of others. Let God be the judge. Are you willing right now to take a step? You can pray that God will help you to put into practice even more of what you know is expected.

It is my prayer that God will hear every one of us and that other people will hear us, too. I pray that we will each begin to receive the promises of God. I pray that each of will feel more intently God's caring for us and sense more clearly ways in which we can express our appreciation to God in our daily walk with Him. Amen.

To choose God is to choose life. To choose life is to choose love.

This passage begins with the words, "See, I have set before you this day life and prosperity, death and adversity." The words Joshua says later are very similar to these. That's not surprising, given that Joshua studied with, learned from and looked up to Moses. You probably remember some of Joshua 24:15, "Now if you are unwilling to serve the Lord, choose this day whom you will serve. . . . but for me and my household, we will serve the Lord." Throughout the Bible, this idea of *choosing* for or against God appears. Adam and Eve chose against God in the Garden. When later they realized how they had been deceived, they reaffirmed their commitment to God, though there were consequences from their earlier choice. Adam and Eve chose to pay attention to what God said; they realized that in so doing, they were choosing life. This is also true for us: Each time we are faced with temptation that has to do with good and evil, we are making a decision to move toward life or death. It isn't always obvious until later, but the decision is always there. We are constantly choosing whether to move toward greater health, life and closeness to God or not. Joshua's question could sound like it is a once-in-a-lifetime decision but really, we make this decision each day.

When David chose to admit his sin to the prophet Nathan, he was choosing life. When Balam chose to listen to God, he was choosing life. When Sarah chose to believe God would fulfill His promise to her, she was choosing life. When you choose to come to church, when you chose to be baptized, when you choose to clean up your language, when you choose to follow the Commandments, when you choose to learn more about what is expected of you, you choose life. When you choose to learn more about the Bible and when you choose to pray, you are choosing life. Each time you choose well, you are choosing life. And each time you make a healthy choice and each time you choose truth, you are choosing to be closer to God.

You may have noticed the struggle that goes on inside of you when you make these kinds of choices. Sometimes it's a big struggle and sometimes it feels like just a little one. Either way, it seldom looks like a clear choice between good and evil, or between life and death. It often seems as if it is a choice between immediate and long-term satisfaction, or between what we want right now and what we are supposed to want. Evil wants us to think of the decision that way, instead of being between good and evil, or between life and death. That's how we can be fooled sometimes. In the Book of Numbers, 12 spies were sent into the Promised Land and told to report what they saw. 10 of the 12 spies interpreted what they saw through a lens of fear and reported that the occupants there were like giants! "We are like grasshoppers to them," they said. Two of the 12 looked through a lens of faith and saw a land filled with milk and honey. So much depends on our perspective!

Did you know that understanding your fears and facing them with faith will transform them? The opposite of this is what evil tries to do: to block us from the Promised Land and its blessings by playing on our fear. When David faced Goliath, he wasn't ignoring the fear. He was letting his faith transform his fear into concentration and trust in God. Fear is not bad; it is letting fear control us that steals our blessings.

One powerful way to let our fears be transformed is by love. We are told in the next verse, " . . . to love the Lord thy God and walk in his ways . . ." Our love and the love we feel from God can transform what we see, how we see it, and how we experience it. When we let God's love for us transform our fears, we can ask such questions as these: How is this fear I feel helping me? God loves me and can use all of my emotions to help me. How does He want to help me through this fear?

Abraham, Isaac, Jacob, Sarah, Rachel and Rebecca chose to go toward God even when they did not know where that would lead them. Just like you when you choose to make changes in your life, they were all going into new territory, replacing old behaviors with new ones. Some of these changes happen subtly and naturally. We find that when we are trying to overcome an addiction, we start choosing new people to hang out with. When we begin to realize we want success in our lives, we find that we want friends going in the same direction we are. We want to be with people who are good examples, who've done or learned the things we want to do or learn.

As you change, you may want to know more about how others have overcome temptations that made them sick. You may want to discover how you too can feel better about yourself. Real change means replacing old behaviors with new behaviors. Ephesians 4:28 says, "Thieves must give up stealing; rather let them labor and work honestly with their hands, so as to have something to share with the needy." In other words, to really change, we want to do more than just halt a bad behavior. We want to replace it with a good one. For example, you can stop using foul language and replace it with good and positive language.

It is my prayer that each of us will be able more easily to choose the good and be able to say with the psalmist, " . . . He makes me lie down in green pastures . . . He guides me in paths of righteousness . . . Surely goodness and mercy shall follow me all the days of my life, and I will dwell in the house of the Lord forever." Amen.

Shame steals innocence. Forgiveness returns it . . . with love.

Genesis can teach us a great deal about ourselves, about evil and temptation, and about our relationship to God. We're first told how man was formed in the dust of the earth and how God breathed life into his nostrils. Our spirit, our very life, is the breath of God. No wonder we feel peace when we are right with God. No wonder we feel clean and right when we get closer to God by reading and studying His word and talking to Him in prayer. The word *atham* means man. The word *adamah* means ground or dust. So these words have the same root. This word relationship reminds us that our bodies are temporary; you are a spirit that temporarily inhabits a body.

This awareness of who we are helps set the stage to be able to view temptation in a new and advantageous way. The word man - *atham* - and earth are all part of the root word for humility. Because it's pride that tricks us into temptation, we're the freest of it when we're the most humble, that is, when we know that we need God. True humility is safe because it turns to God and away from evil. The only way temptation can trick us is by getting us to forget our true identity. Temptation tries to get us to believe that we need this thing or activity in order to be complete. The truth is that when we know we need God and we have a close relationship to Him, we feel complete. And we are not so easily tempted.

As we see in Genesis, when evil tempts us, it will be with sly, shrewd and crafty temptations that almost always sound sensible at the time. (The word subtle here also means crafty, sly and sensible.) In chapter 3, we read that the serpent was subtler than any other wild creature the Lord had made. This is a major tip. Temptation usually begins to work on us just this way—very subtly. But even when both sides of an argument sound sensible, only one will be based on obedience to God's rules for our lives. This is how we tell the difference.

The pattern that evil uses to attempt to trick us has not changed since Adam and Eve's time. Another tip-off we have when encountering temptation has to do with who is talking to us. We often get clues about someone being a snake. One of the signs for Eve was when the snake magnified God's requirements. He said, "Did God say you shall not eat of any tree in the garden?" God had only prohibited one tree, the tree of good and evil. The snake implied that God would never make such a harsh rule. He also subtly implied that Eve had already broken the rule since she had already eaten from the other trees. Evil likes to overemphasize the rules until they sound ridiculous. Then we become more vulnerable because we feel we might fall short or not fit into these rules.

At first, Eve did not understand what was going on. Temptation may, indeed, come from someone who claims to love us. The snake certainly acted like Eve's friend. Sometimes, these people even believe that they love us. We have all met persuasive people whom we later realized were snakes who had only their own interests at heart.

The second major mistake Eve made was in arguing with evil. Evil likes it when we argue with it, because then it can use our words against us. Jesus knew this and, in arguing with evil, did not use his own words. He used words from Scripture. Our own words make us more vulnerable because evil is not restrained by the truth. Twisting our words to mean something we didn't mean is part of the trick.

The snake deliberately misled Eve during the argument into accepting a lie. The lie was that she and Adam would be like God and thus would know good from evil. Evil often tricks us just this way, by sounding sincere, as if God was involved and sanctioned the sin. Here the snake used a legitimate desire to be more like God as a way to make the sin seem more desirable. A part of the trickery was some truth mixed with the lie. It was pleasant to look at the fruit. It looked like it would taste good. Evil narrows our perspective by getting us to focus on just how something looks to our senses and to our flesh, and not how it looks to our spirit.

The end result for Eve and Adam being tricked was shame instead of God-like glory. This is how it always goes, shame following sin. This is how evil works. Then shameful feelings can even infect others to feel shame. And when we feel shame, there are really only three things we can do about it. We can ignore it, deny that it means much to us, or do more than we did in the past. Sinners sometimes commit more sin because then they don't feel as badly about the earlier sin. They have new sin to think about. This is one way in which evil works. It wants the bad to grow.

However, we can stop this pattern. We can confess it to God and receive forgiveness. Forgiveness protects us, insulates us, and gives us a new clean slate. Forgiveness frees us from the bondage of sin that sin generates.

It is my prayer that whatever shame or remembered sins occur to you today, you will give to God in prayer and let yourself feel more and more forgiven and accepted. I pray that you realize God created you in a special way and you really are someone special. Amen.

Being alone is radically different from being lonely.

Exodus 24: 12 reads, "The Lord said to Moses, 'Come up to me on the mountain and wait there . . . '" Moses, who was already close to God, was called up to a mountaintop experience with Him. Many of us, too, have been called to an alone time with God. Yet for many of us, we equate being alone—a time when we can feel closest to God—with being lonely. They are *very* different.

When we are lonely, we feel sorry for ourselves and want the loneliness to end as quickly as possible because it is so painful. Some of us have feared loneliness so much that we have done almost anything to avoid it. We have stayed with people we did not like or who treated us badly just to have someone to ward off the loneliness. If we really think about it, most of the sins we have committed were a way to avoid loneliness, weren't they? Why did we lie? Wasn't it to keep people from rejecting us? We told what we thought someone wanted to hear so we could avoid rejection and therefore (we thought) feel less lonely. When we stole we were trying to avoid facing our loneliness. Some may have tricked themselves into thinking it was only for drugs but one of the key reasons people use drugs is that they do not want to feel the hurt of loneliness, especially that involving rejection by their families.

It is our alone time, when, just like Moses, we can feel close to God. Alone times can be pivotal in a person's transformation from living a life filled with sin to living a life close to God. I knew in the prison that some people used the alone time that cellblock provided to experience a sense of closeness to God. It slows you down enough to get you to really look at yourself and your past. Being aware of your sin with no place to run and hide means you want to talk with God about what you did and did not do. I have seen people change dramatically while they were in cellblock. They examined their lives with God and decided they wanted to change. One woman said, "I slept as much as a could, and then I still had to face my past and what I did." She said, "I desperately wanted to feel clean and be able to start over." She did.

It's ironic that so many of us have spent so much time avoiding the very thing that could change our lives. Sin and evil know that when we're alone with God, they are not invited. Having alone time with God raises our self-esteem and gives us the Spirit's gift of self-control. Being lonely without God lowers our self-esteem; we begin thinking that there is something wrong with us that we're so lonely. So we become more vulnerable to committing sin. Being alone with God is anything but. When we feel close to God, we feel connected to something much bigger than ourselves. We feel loved and we feel protected. There's no room for loneliness in this equation.

So how does God raise our self-esteem and self-control? He gives us the Ten Commandments. As with Moses, when we really receive the Commandments and recognize that God gave them to us for our own good, we can begin to appreciate these rules a little more. The Ten Commandments are designed to enhance our lives individually and collectively. Breaking them brings pain and trouble. Following them brings more peace. The Commandments are the contract—the Covenant—between God and us. When we agree to abide by His rules, we live in His house and peace reigns in our lives.

Now I'd like to add the topic of forgiveness to our equation. As Christians, we believe that we can live best with the Commandments through Jesus Christ. This is because we can lighten our load through being forgiven. When someone is lonely, they may well be aware of their mistakes, flaws and sins, but he or she will not feel forgiven. They will feel condemned, punished, worthless and needy. No sense of forgiveness there. But when someone spends time alone with God, they can feel cleansed and forgiven. No wonder when some folks came out of cellblock they were new people—able to meet new challenges and to feel good. It is really the same with prison in general.

No matter what we have done or thought, we can be forgiven and move closer to God. Are you willing to let God transform your loneliness? Are you willing to have the mountaintop experience? Instead of only telling God what you want, are you willing to spend time in prayer seeking to discover what or how you can improve? Even when others are around us, we have many, many moments that we can spend in prayer and sense God's presence. We do not always have to get into a posture that lets everyone know we are praying. We can pray while walking, while working, waiting or during study breaks and lunch break. Seeking those alone times is how you have been growing on the inside of you. It is God's Word that is alive and active. When we take His Word into our hearts and minds, it changes us.

It is my prayer that each of us will sense more intensely in the days to come ways in which God is showing us that we are cared about and loved. Amen.

61

You Can Be Forgiven And Cleansed
            2 Sam 5:1-5, Eph 5: 8-14, Jn 9:1-11

They became the best of friends . . .

This passage is about a major event but is reported in a matter-of-fact
way. As Biblical passages go, it is not one we might ordinarily study in
order to receive blessings. We might even overlook it. Yet if we allow the
Holy Spirit to enlighten us, all of Scripture is good for study, instruction and
encouragement. Even the seemingly insignificant events of our lives can
lead us to big discoveries if we are willing to be led by God.

The logical completion of what began much earlier and many small
discoveries led to the event recorded here: the tribes coming to David to
affirm him as their king. The people believed that it was God who was
ordaining David as the King of Israel. They knew that Samuel had
anointed him, even when Saul was alive. They also knew that God's hand
seemed to be on David, for he had escaped death many times as he
repeatedly and successfully fought Israel's enemies. The tribes had
repeated evidence of God's endorsement of David in the events leading
up this coronation day. When it is true that God is directing us, there will
be similar collaborating evidence along the way.

So why did God choose David? He was the youngest son of Jesse; the
shortest and least physically handsome; he did not look the part, did not
come from a royal family and was not rich. By the world's standards, he
was not the right man. And how could God choose David, knowing that
later he would commit adultery and murder? David was not a very good
father, even if he had been a good shepherd. Yet God said David was a
man after his own heart. David's faith was impressive. When he was
wrong, he could and would admit it. When he was forgiven, he believed it
and acted upon being forgiven. He learned how to have God as a best
friend and was able to continue that relationship when he was king. He
confessed his sin and called on God. He did not consult his astrological
sign, care about and read his horoscope, call the 900 number psychics,
decide what to do based on what was fashionable, rely on self-serving
people for advice, or take polls to know what to do. He was interested in
what God wanted.

Yes, David was a great witness for God. Because of his faith, he was
forgiven and became an even more powerful witness. One way you know
this transformation was real is because David stopped his sin. Never denying
it, he repented and accepted God's forgiveness. When we really know we
are forgiven, cared about and accepted, we are free from the sin we were
struggling with in the first place. A person who only temporarily stops does
not really know forgiveness. If they did, the struggle would lessen.

You know, it's not that we become such moral giants. Rather, it is that when you really let in God's forgiveness and acceptance, the desire is taken away. You become a new person. As a shepherd, David had learned how not to be lonely when being alone. He learned how to call upon God and be best friends with Him. He had perhaps learned what the New Testament calls praying without ceasing. He learned to rely on God's presence. What God did with David, He will do with us as well for God works through our faith.

Sometimes, it is easier for us to see God's endorsement of someone else than it is for us to see how God wants to bless us. Our own doubts get in the way. If God wants to bless you, it is also so someone else can get blessed. We know this when there are multiple signs and when other believers confirm our belief. It is right for us to support what we believe is God's initiative. This is one way we get blessed and can then help others.

We can remember that our God can transform us no matter what our background. God transformed a shepherd to become a shepherd king. He transformed fishermen to become fishers of men. He transformed Rehab the prostitute from someone who was scorned to a heroine of faith. She was remembered, celebrated and admired even by the highest society. Because of Mary Magdalene's faith, she was transformed from a psychiatric patient and prostitute to a celebrated and respected evangelist. She even married an important church leader. God can transform your past. If you were abused, if you stole, lied, coveted, or defamed holy things, if you struggled with your anger, shame, or pride, God can transform you and your background. Why does God like to transform us so much? Why does God not want only people who are kept clean throughout their lives? It is because only accepting the ones who have never greatly sinned ignores the grace and the power of His forgiveness. It is right that Jesus is in line with David because he took the idea of forgiveness to the ultimate conclusion. Real forgiveness is God's medicine for sin.

Friends, it is my prayer that each of us would draw so close to God that we can each feel His forgiveness. I pray that we can each testify to God's power that it can work through us. I pray that people will see how God is transforming us and we will boldly want what we have and are receiving. Amen.

62

Making Today A Spiritual Day
Jn 19: 17-30; Isa 52:13, 53: 1-12; Heb 4: 14-16, 5: 7-9

Friday—and every day—is a good day for worship.

The passages in John illustrate the contrast between a spiritual and a "world view" of life. On the one hand, you have the inscription, "Jesus of Nazareth, King of the Jews," meaning that Jesus was a king, in the most profound sense. On the other hand, from the world's point of view, the inscription was meant to be terribly degrading and insulting to Jesus, suggesting that he was a fool.

Tradition has it that only the disciple he loved; Mary, Jesus' mother; his mother's sister; and Mary Magdalene were at the foot of the cross. The others who loved him stayed away. They were afraid, indifferent or uninformed of the event. In contrast to Mary and John were the soldiers, doing their terrible jobs, and a group comprising indifferent or jeering onlookers. Some other onlookers may have watched the execution in horror. They had loved this prophet and had hoped he would do great things. Now here he was, being executed in the style reserved by the Romans for the lowest of the low.

The soldiers and the mocking crowd couldn't see anything spiritual about Jesus or about that day. They were indifferent to Jesus' pain, to Mary's and to that of the other two men being crucified. The soldiers were so indifferent; they were focused on gambling for Jesus' clothes. When people can't see the spiritual, there is nothing we can do to make them see it. They have to be willing to ask God to help them see, to ask God for guidance. The soldiers were not willing to do this, nor were the indifferent onlookers. In addition to his intense physical pain, Jesus must have felt the pain of this indifference. It's often easier to have someone angry with us than to have them ignore us, especially when we are suffering.

Jesus would have been aware, though, of Scripture being fulfilled. He would have been aware of the spiritual meaning of what he was doing and of what the crowd was doing. The emotional pain of being treated indifferently may have been diminished by his attention to what was being fulfilled, as Scripture had predicted. When we see signs of prophecies coming true, it can bring a comfort.

It is in Jesus' response to the crowd's mocking and the people and soldiers' indifference that we see an awesome contrast to a worldview. In Jesus' place, many people would have shouted angrily, cursed or mocked the mockers to get back at them. Some would have cursed the soldiers to entice them to at least take notice. What Jesus did in the midst of his intense pain, loss and loneliness was a profound act of kindness and love that can only bring us to our knees. No greater contrast between the two ways of doing things could have been drawn.

Looking to his mother and the disciple he loved at the foot of the cross, Jesus said, "Woman, behold your son!" To the disciple, he said, "Behold your mother!" Jesus spoke to the two people who cared the most about him. In love, he prepared them for his departure. Under any circumstances and perhaps most when we know we are going away, it takes a lot of love to give to another the care of someone we love. Many of the prison inmates had to do this. They had had to place children with others to love them and care for them in their absence. You may have had to do this, too. This is love.

To be spiritual means to be more concerned about spiritual matters than material ones. Jesus' act of giving his mother a new son and his disciple a new mother was that type of spiritual awareness. To be spiritual means to be concerned about another's feelings, to care for and to love others. To be indifferent, to not care, to be able to numb up and create indifference occurs when a person has his or her focus on something that isn't God. The indifference of the soldiers is what the world gives. Everything is about, "What's in it for me?" Spirituality is about caring for the rights and feelings of others and knowing that you can't out-give God. He can give you more love than you can give away. To be spiritual means you choose to do what you know is right even if your flesh tells you to do something else. It means listening more to what God says than to what your feelings say. Our feelings follow our actions. Good actions bring good feelings. Waiting for good feelings without changing negative actions may mean waiting a long time.

Good Friday isn't a happy day, but maybe it is a good day. It is a day that can inspire us to be good, to seek good, to be drawn to the good. Jesus said that no one can serve two masters. When you treat others well, you are doing what Jesus told you to do. You are serving God. We are to do unto others as we would have them do unto us. When you treat people well because of your love and appreciation of God, it is worship. When you treat others well because God told you to, even though you don't like them and perhaps they don't like you, you are doing it for Christ's sake. Your act of kindness is an act of worship and witness. Every act of genuine kindness by a believer is an act of worship.

The real question of today isn't what is good about Good Friday, but what good can you do on Good Friday? How can you allow this day to be filled with the goodness that God is giving you? Jesus said, "Seek and ye shall find, knock and the door shall be opened unto you, ask and it shall be given." What you seek, you will find. Thank God you can choose good this Friday. It is my prayer that we all do. Amen.

Spiritual eyes see grace.

On Easter, we celebrate the empty tomb and Jesus' resurrection from the dead. This event more than 2000 years ago was so transforming that thereafter, the disciples stood firm in their beliefs about the risen Christ, even in the face of persecution and death. (All but John were executed. He was thrown in prison.) The same people who were so scared before the Crucifixion were all willing to die for their faith after seeing the risen Lord. Many other people not mentioned in the Bible were similarly martyred for their beliefs. Why? Perhaps they had seen the effect of faith on a loved one. Perhaps they knew a person whom Jesus had healed. In any event, their faith was so strong that they were willing to die for it. They were transformed by what they had seen and experienced both during Jesus' life and by what happened afterward.

Mary Magdalene is a good example of transformation. Before meeting Jesus and being healed, Mary Magdalene was a woman with severe mental problems who supported herself with prostitution. Like many people who have been abused, she probably blamed herself. These people tell themselves their shame is because of their sin and they often engage in self-destructive behaviors. Yet they seldom know that feeling shame or guilt is a sign of possible redemption. When Mary Magdalene met Jesus, he helped her to feel clean and accepted. Her transformation was probably dramatic. It always is when you let go of the shame from the past and accept forgiveness.

Jesus said Mary loved much because she had been forgiven much. Because she was willing to feel forgiven, she received more love and could love more. Love comes from God. And when we are able to feel His forgiveness, we feel more of His love. It is the key that helped Mary to have the faith to believe, to change and to be healed. When people profess their faith and pledge to change, they miss the point. It isn't what we do that produces the change. Change comes when we allow and invite God into our lives.

Mary was the first evangelist after the Resurrection - not just because she delivered the news of Jesus' resurrection that morning, but because she let her life demonstrate God's power to transform us. Her change was permanent. You may know someone whose life is different because of his or her faith. You may already be like Mary Magdalene. You may already be a walking witness for the Lord. Your life and your gentleness, your honesty and your continued willingness to change at God's direction are all signs of God's presence in your life.

But we don't have an empty tomb or a miracle . . . or do we? Some people look back on history and ask, "If there really were miracles then do we not see them today?" And yet anyone who wants to see miracles today can see them. Some of you are living miracles. Every time an addict really flees from the addiction, a miracle occurs. Every time a person is freed from a shameful past so they are willing to open the whole closet and let it all out, a miracle occurs. When you are able to let go of those old secrets because you feel forgiven and accepted by God, that's a miracle.

Most miracles don't happen all at once. Neither do children begin to walk all at once. First, they squirm on their backs, then they scoot, then they crawl either forward or backward, and then they stand. When we expect someone to change from sin to spirituality overnight, we are being unrealistic. When we look at each other through spiritual eyes that include grace, everything changes.

When the disciples ran to the tomb that morning, Peter slowed down. I think it was the guilt of having denied Jesus three times that caused him to do this. John didn't have guilt in denying Jesus, but he saw him die, so he may have just stopped at the entrance, remembering. Peter would have been afraid not of Jesus' absence, but of facing him. Like many of us, he struggled with forgiveness.

Many of us have struggled with certain sins. Some of us have struggled with ones we seem unable to overcome. We promise, we pledge, and we mean it. Then we still do what we promised we wouldn't do. We sometimes wonder how often we will be forgiven but forgiveness isn't the reward for putting sin out of our lives. It is the medicine for it in the first place. In other words, God's forgiveness is what gives us the strength, courage and ability to give up sin in the first place. When we develop a personal relationship with the risen Lord and we understand the transformation this can bring about, we begin to change. People today who have seen Him or felt His presence are seldom the same. They change. There is no doubt for them forever after. They know they have experienced a miracle.

If we haven't changed as much as we believe we should, let's talk to God about it. If you still struggle with an obvious sin, let's let God take care of it for you. Perhaps you aren't ready yet to put the sin behind you. When you know that you are loved either way, it becomes easier to stop. It feels so good when we are freed from some sin. We start to feel alive and happy, and to feel hope. You can feel this way.

It is my prayer that today we can all let a little more of God's hope and faith into our hearts. I pray that we let more people see the change present in us and that we praise God for His blessings. Amen.

Loving the *Agape* Way
Jn 21: 15-19, Rev 5: 11-14, Acts 5: 27-32

"Feed my sheep, tend my lambs and feed my sheep."

After breakfast, Jesus asked Peter, "Do you love me more than these?" Peter's response was, "Yes, Lord, you know that I love you." Peter's words have a beautiful tone to them but he really did not understand what Jesus was asking. Did Jesus mean, "Do you love me more than these fish you caught?" If so, implied in Jesus' question is some request for Peter to reaffirm his commitment to being a fisher of men, rather than a fisherman. Did he mean, "Do you love me more than your brothers, the disciples?" Peter didn't really recognize the implied request for reaffirming his commitment to follow Jesus.

We often hear what we have been accustomed to hearing, instead of what God or others are really saying. Sometimes we are starved for attention and we look for compliments. Sometimes, we're so used to being criticized that that's what we hear. In Peter's case, he jumped at hearing in the question a comparison between him and the other disciples. But when we compare ourselves to others, we almost always lose. If we puff ourselves up and say, "I'm better than she is," our self-congratulations will be short lived, as it sets us up to be controlled by our pride. We'll end up following our pride rather than what's best for us. If we compare ourselves to others and feel that we come up short, we still lose because we end up feeling badly about ourselves.

None of us can possibly know if we love God more than others do. An honest and insightful answer to Jesus' question would have addressed this and answered with humility. "Lord, I don't know if my love for you is more than their love for you. I do love you." Jesus may also have been implying to Peter that he wanted him to love the other disciples. If Peter had heard this question, he would have realized that our love for the Lord is reflected in whether we are loving toward others. If you can't love others, you can't love God. If you have barriers to loving others, those blocks are also there between you and God. The way to improve your relationship with God is to work on the blocks you have to loving others.

This passage really has to do with the difference between two kinds of love. The English translation doesn't reflect these very well. Jesus asked Peter, "Do you *agape* me?" and Peter answered, "You know I *philos* you." These two different Greek words for love reflect radically different meanings. Jesus asked, "Do you have desire for my good? Do you have loyalty to me and do you affirm me in your mind? Do you understand me?" When we love in an *agape* way, there isn't the emotion of love, but rather a commitment to a standard of value for other human beings. When we *agape* people we do not like and even our enemies, we want good for them because we follow God. It means we want God's purpose in their lives.

To have *philos* love is to have the emotion of brotherly love, a powerful emotion of connection. And while this is very nice, emotion comes and goes. It is fickle. It comes and goes, and we can't manufacture it just because we want to. We get confused sometimes thinking that *philos* love for a person means they will always have our best interest at heart. But it is *agape* love that we can really count on. John 3:16 describes *agape* love: "For God so loved the world that he gave his only begotten Son . . ."

We, too, can hear what Jesus tells Peter. If we love God, we are to feed His sheep. Again, the English doesn't illustrate very well the different meanings conveyed by Jesus' words. In some translations, the words are rendered, "Feed my sheep, tend my lambs, and feed my sheep." We are to feed Jesus' sheep in many ways: spiritually, physically, emotionally and morally. I know that many of you show a nurturing attitude toward others who need that support. It means a lot to us spiritually to sense the support of others.

When I worked in the prison system, I often heard about this person or that person who inspired others, encouraging them to read their Bibles, to study, to be baptized and to respect God's commandments. Isn't it interesting that the women who reached out to others with *agape* love were the ones who almost never returned to the institution? When you set your sights on assisting, nurturing and helping others, you get blessed. You can't out-give God.

Do you love Jesus? He is asking each of us the question, "Do you love me? Then feed my sheep, tend my lambs, and feed my sheep." We can demonstrate to Him that we do love Him by showing our works of kindness and spiritual encouragement to others. I challenge you this week to show your faith by reaching out in an *agape* way toward someone. Let him or her sense your faith and your commitment to God. Encourage him or her in some way so that they can feel God's love and care.

It is my prayer that each of us would so let God's love for us in, that, in turn, we become even more eager to nurture other Christians. Whether they are young or old, beginners or longtime veterans of faith, they all need nurturing. Amen.

If we don't reach out to others, who will?

There is a message in this verse that can be a little disturbing at first. It has to do with responsibility. It is in what Jesus said that evening, in verse 23: "If you forgive the sins of any, they are forgiven; if you retain the sins of any, they are retained." There is something to celebrate here, but we also begin to see the responsibility that goes with our faith. It is wonderful to be given power or ability. It is also a huge responsibility. If the church (church with a small "c" means all believers) and the church only has the ability on Earth to forgive, then condemning the church and judging it makes people unable to be forgiven. As representatives of the church, how we behave may make the difference as to whether people come into the church and thus, can be forgiven. Let's explore this idea further.

When the disciples were huddled together that first evening, they were afraid. Even though they had seen the empty tomb and Mary had told them that Jesus was alive, they were afraid. Perhaps they characterize us. Just like the disciples that evening, we also struggle with fear, doubt, and other human emotions that seem to get in our way. We want encouragement. We believe yet we also struggle with belief. Sometimes, we find ourselves doubting and then we're embarrassed to admit to others and to ourselves that we struggle with doubt.

But we all struggle with lots of human emotions. We struggle with doing what we know we shouldn't do and not doing what we know we should do. We can remember that what the church says has real and eternal power. When Thomas separated, he didn't get the blessing he would have gotten with the church, the group of believers. It was only when he was back with the other believers that he was blessed with Jesus appearing to him as well. That is not to say that God does not appear to us personally or privately. Of course He does. It means that people cannot separate themselves from the church and continue to receive the benefits and carry out the responsibilities that we have. This was Jesus' message to the disciples that evening: We need the support of the church. We belong in the church, the community of believers. This is where we receive forgiveness and blessings. This is where our faith can receive support.

Now, more on this responsibility issue. Jesus made it clear that we have a responsibility to make the church as attractive and inviting as possible. This is especially true about our actions around people who are not part of any church. It is when they commit themselves to the church that their sins can be forgiven. If they are condemned because we didn't invite them in or help them to feel invited, included or accepted, we will be held accountable.

With power goes responsibility. One of the commandments is to honor the Sabbath day. Some churches honor God on Sunday, some on Saturday, some with music, some with only singing. Some churches worship with much emotion displayed as part of the services and some display little emotion. They are all part of the church. Jesus worshipped with other believers. The church was very important to him. He gave the Holy Spirit to the church—to the community of believers—not just to select individuals.

When we invite people in to the church, we're not recruiting for any particular church or denomination. We're inviting people in to a community of faith. We have an obligation to invite and to encourage, making the church accessible. Our allegiance to God is displayed in our faith as demonstrated to others. Our hospitality to others helps them become forgiven. If you appreciate that a believer took the time to care enough about you to bring you into the church, then you owe it to the one who helped you to pass that encouragement on to others.

Is there someone to whom you owe an apology? Then pay it because that debt may be standing in that person's path to the church. Is there someone whom you haven't treated very well? Ask that person's forgiveness and clear the path for that person to worship with you. Is there someone you know who is blocked from being a part of the church because he or she has been hurt? It is part of your obligation to reach out to that person as the representative of the church and to encourage, assist, and make amends for the church if need be. Sometimes we need to apologize for the actions of the church toward others. We are God's representatives. We have an obligation and a duty to each other and to God to reach out.

There are many people who are incarcerated by sin and who have little or no knowledge of the church, belief, or the Bible. There are also many people who are burdened by shame from harsh interpretations of Scripture. If we don't reach out to them, who will? The church has the ability to forgive. The church is like a hospital for faith, for belief, and for forgiveness. All of us have the responsibility to extend that help to others.

It is my prayer that each of us receives so much comfort and encouragement that we find ourselves easily reaching out to others. I pray that we especially feel, sense, and see how important we are to God. Amen.

Choosing the Right Flock
Jn 1: 1-10, 1 Pet 2: 19-25, Acts 2: 36-41

Sheep often hurt themselves when they follow other sheep instead of the Shepherd.

Most of us want to be able to know when someone is speaking God's truth. We want (and need) to be in line with God and His truth but we're not sure we have a good radar detector on these matters. We wonder sometimes if we are being tricked by what's popular, persuasive, new or generally accepted. We may wonder where we belong and how we can assess the "rightness" of a person, a church, a group or a denomination. How can we know when people really care for us and when they simply want to use us? How can we tell when they are carrying the Word of God to us and when they are carrying their own words or the words of the ultimate thief?

This passage says the sheep hear His voice and know Him. His sheep will follow Him. In other words, if you are God's child, you will know His voice. You will know the truth of it and you will want to follow Him. So the first question is: Am I God's child? This question can be asked other ways: To whom do you belong? To whom are you related and who are your bothers and sisters?

All of these questions come down to whether you have a personal relationship with God or not; whether you want to be a part of God's loving family. One easy way to know whose side you are on (and whose side anyone else is on) is by applying the fruits of the Spirit. If there is more peace, joy, gentleness, kindness, love, humility and self-control in your life than anger, bitterness, selfishness, envy, drunkenness, impurity and fornication, you are okay! You know who your shepherd is. Scripture is clear about this point. When we really have a relationship with God, the fruits of the Spirit begin to appear and the fruits of the flesh disappear. If someone shows anger, envy, bitterness and bad habits, the fruits of the Spirit are in short supply.

Often, especially when you are committed to God, you sense the truth when you hear it. When something is "off," you may have a deep, intuitive feeling telling you this. There are things that can interfere with our "truth detector," though. Sin and temptation can distort things. Mature Christians know that when they are tempted, they need to be careful. The information coming in from their detectors can be less clear.

Where religion is concerned, if we're used to being criticized, people who tell us they are religious and are damning, judgmental and condemning really can sound religious. Many of us have felt so bad and so shameful that almost anyone who was critical of us seemed to be telling the truth. We didn't trust praise and believed only criticism. Jesus said that He came to bring us life and more abundant life. God wants us to have the good stuff—the *real* good stuff.

We can apply this "positive meter" to our desire to change things in our lives. People who want to lose weight, stop smoking, quit a bad habit, start a good habit or become religious often make a similar mistake. They try to shame themselves into good behavior. "I'm going to force myself." "I'll do it this time. I should have done it long ago." One reason these approaches don't work and won't work is that they use the wrong fruit. God and His love are not included. When you begin a task that is right for you, which would help you be healthier and is closer to God's Word, do you first ask God if now is even the right time, if you have enough tools to accomplish the task? Do you ask God if you are even ready to begin?

"Everyone who hears these words of mine and does them will be like a wise person who built a house upon rock; the rain fell and the floods came and the winds blew and beat on the house, but it did not fail because it had been founded on rock." We begin by accepting a truth. Twelve step programs refer to this truth as admitting our powerlessness. Admitting we are powerless and that God can do it is an act of worship. People who do this are often amazed at how easy change becomes.

We can include God right at the beginning. If you want to make changes in your life, talk to God about it first. As a Christian, the first step we take in deciding directions for our lives is to consult God about the timing, the planning and the foundation. If you feel that God has been telling you to make some changes, talk to Him about it. Find out what His Word says. After you have searched the Bible for what God says, ask Him what comes next. One important way to pray is simply to wait for God to speak to us.

People who are going to be successful living on the outside or successful bringing about real changes find a change in the type of people to whom they are drawn. If you want to stop cursing, stop smoking or behaving dishonestly—and God is truly with you in making this change—you will find yourself making new friends of people who are making the changes you want to make. And when we are sincere about following God's Word, we start finding ourselves drawn to people who already are following it. We want to be with other sheep that belong to the Shepherd.

It is my prayer that something we hear today from the Holy Spirit will help each of us to become closer to God so we can know more of the abundant life He wants for us. I especially pray that we would ask God with humility and kindness to help us to see. Amen.

"Love one another as I have loved you."

Jesus spoke to his disciples. He told them—and is telling us—a spiritual truth: If we love him, we will keep God's commandments. What does this mean? It means we will want to please Him. It means that we will accept that we need to follow God's commandments, and that we will accept them as the real boundaries in our lives. We will let Him be the authority and have the final word in our lives. People who refuse to accept God's values are blocked from being able to really love since all real love comes from God. Sin separates us from the truth, from God and from real love.

This is a truth that the world has difficulty understanding. The physical world does not really understand love, and gives it a meaning that has little to do with God's meaning. In the world, love often means lust. It may mean to own, manipulate and exploit. It may mean physical attraction. The word Jesus used here for love is *agape*. This kind of love is one of intelligence, reason and understanding. It wants good for us. This type of love is patient, kind and does not want to exploit or use, but to give and assist and care for. The world often does not understand this way of loving God or loving each other. With this kind of love, you can love your mother and father, even with their shortcomings, even if they were abusive. With this kind of love, you can even love your enemies. Quite a concept!

It might be helpful to understand the different ways people have of not acknowledging or of disobeying God's laws. The first level describes people of limited ability—they are mentally, emotionally or socially disabled. They do not have the ability to function well, and they can't teach their children what they don't know. Their mistakes are understandable. As adults we can understand and forgive people who are doing the very best they know how to do.

The second level includes people who are incredibly naïve. These people do not really understand sin. They had no training, no nurturing to use as an example, and had to grow up the best way they could. These people are fully capable of learning, and break commandments more out of ignorance than out of a sinful nature.

The third level includes those who break the commandments because the commandments are not as important to them as what they want. They may not want to hurt their children, but their feelings and wants always come first. They may even feel a bit badly that their children are hurt as a result of their sins, but it doesn't stop them. These people can't really love because their lives are guided by their feelings, not by commitments. Their so-called love does not even recognize the hurt that it causes.

The fourth level involves those who not only knowingly break the commandments, but who get secret pleasure from rebelling against them and from hurting others. This type of person is very cruel. They exploit, use and neglect, and they secretly enjoy causing pain. They may say they regret causing hurt, but given the opportunity, they do it again and again.

If you recognize either of your parent's behavior or your own behavior in any of these examples, praise God—especially if you want to change or understand rather than blame. Love causes us to change, like a plant turning to the sun. The more ability we have to love, the less sin will be seen in us. The more sin, the less ability we have to show love.

One woman I knew when I was a prison chaplain fell into the third group. She was only marginally sorry for the major hurts she had caused. She responded first and foremost to her own desires. She had spent a long time breaking rules and hurting people, including herself. One day when her child was visiting her, the child said, "Mom, how come you like drugs and doing wrong more than you like me?" Those words must have broken through her denial and convicted her heart of her sins. She started to change. The next day she began looking and acting better. She stopped the dishonesty and began applying herself to school and to changing. People wondered what had come over her. She made a 180-degree turn.

This woman was feeling good guilt. Good guilt makes us want to change. (Bad guilt just makes us feel badly about stuff we can't change.) The words of the child whose mother I told you about echoed Jesus' words: If you love me, you will come home to me. The world will not acknowledge that we must choose. The world says, "Go ahead. No one will know." The world says," It won't hurt anyone but you." The world lies. We cannot have it both ways. Do we want to be able to love? Do we want to not hurt the ones we say we love? "If you love me, you will keep my commandments."

Do you want this day to begin with a new way to love? Do you want to make amends, to be forgiven, to be reminded of how forgiven you are? Then recognize that if you feel remorse for your actions, God is still encouraging you.

It is my prayer that today you become able to feel God's love for you so much that you are filled with an awareness of His presence casting out your loneliness. Amen.

68

God Wants To Bless You
                Jn 14: 1-12, Acts 6: 1-7, 1 Pet 2: 4-10

Believing in God means that we can be blessed.

This passage begins with the words, "Do not let your hearts be troubled. Believe in God, believe in me." The word *troubled* means to cause commotion, to lose one's spirit to fear and dread, to become anxious or distressed, or to have doubts. What do all of us fret the most about? Am I loved? Does my mother love me? Do my children love me? Does my friend love me? Is there anyone who loves me? Is there enough love for me?

If we really admit it, we are afraid of this terrible loneliness. We want to feel connected and cared about. Who among us hasn't felt afraid of being rejected? Who among us hasn't said, done, thought and been afraid of doing really dumb things because we knew how terrible our fear of loneliness was? Many of us have used drugs, work, business, sex and schemes—anything—to avoid loneliness. We have lied, cheated, stolen . . . and still we were jealous, envious and hurt because we didn't think that we were loved enough.

The Bible tells us here that we can stop all that when we believe. At first reading, it almost seems like we are being insulted or criticized for not believing. Nothing is farther from the truth. We are being given a real gift: We're being told about a path, a door, a way that we didn't know existed. We have the ability to end the hurt, the pain, and anguish we have felt in our hearts. Not only do we have the ability to stop it, God wants us to. He doesn't want us to feel the awful turmoil of worry, torment, anguish, sorrow and loneliness. He wants us to feel cared about, blessed, loved and accompanied by a great friend. Through believing in God, we can end the turmoil in our hearts. In fact, when we look to the points of pain, we know where we can apply the cure. It's like putting balm on a wound. We can believe that God wants us to receive His blessings. Real belief means accepting God's healing love.

To not believe in something is impossible. We're always relying on some kind of belief. For instance, someone can say they do not believe in God. What they're saying indirectly is that they rely on their experience in this physical world. Something or someone is going to be of ultimate importance in their lives. It may be a person, a pleasure, the avoidance of pain, or the achievement of some goal. The problem is that anything or anyone besides God that we put in the ultimate place in our lives will cause us pain. Whatever we place above God in our lives hurts us. If it is someone else's love, our fear of losing it tears at us. If it is being alone, that fear will tear at us. Only God will give us steadfast and enduring, unending love.

We are told here to believe in God and to also believe in Jesus. *To believe* means, "to trust in." It means to commit ourselves. It means to believe God's Words and to put trust in what God says in the Bible. When we do that, we are blessed. Abraham believed God's Words to him. Genesis15: 6 reads, "And he believed the Lord; and the Lord reckoned it to him as righteousness." Throughout the Bible there is reward for believing in God. It protects us from sin and its consequences. Believing in God means that we can be blessed. Abraham, Joseph, Daniel, Moses, Sarah, Esther, Mary, Ruth. . . . the list of people delivered from trouble through faith is long. God blesses us through belief. Jesus said about his hometown that he could do little for the people there because of their lack of belief. It almost seems as if belief is the electrical cord that the blessing of electricity passes through to reach us.

Belief in God's Word has more practical, everyday rewards than miracles could bring us. It helps us with tragedy, gives us guidelines to keep us safe, and shows us how to have the happiest and most rewarding lives. Hebrews says that the Bible is living and active. Beliefs change how we see yet our beliefs change what we *can* see.

So how do we do this? How do we increase our belief so that our hearts are not troubled? Hebrews 11:6 says," And without faith it is impossible to please God, for whoever would approach him must believe that he exists and he rewards those who seek him." How do we increase our belief? Act on the belief that God rewards those people who diligently seek Him. Here, "diligently" implies that people who work hard at seeking God will be rewarded. We have to put forth effort.

Winners go toward the fear. Why? It is because it is putting faith in God to approach the things that we have been afraid of. Are you afraid of being alone? Then trust God enough to help you cope with the loneliness and to provide you with relief. Are you afraid of the feelings you feel around your family? Facing those feelings with God's help will transform them. Whatever we are afraid of—whether it is life, death or anything in between—we when we go ahead and face it by trusting God's Word,we win. Like Paul, we can say that we are more than winners. We are conquerors. We can do all things through Christ, who strengthens us.

It is my prayer that each of us will begin to allow the pain to direct us where we can apply belief in our lives. It is my prayer especially that each of us feels God's love so powerfully that we can let ourselves be comforted and feel loved today and everyday. Amen.

69

Giving Glory to God
Acts 1: 12-14, 1 Pet 4: 12-19, Jn 17: 1-11

To whom or what do your actions give glory?

One message that jumps out in this passage concerns glory. Jesus' request to God for glory is amazingly unselfish. Jesus was asking God for the glory that would go with his being crucified so his disciples would have eternal life. He wanted all of us to be blessed.

Can you imagine praying for others, many of whom you don't know, when your own terribly painful execution is close at hand? Many of us know only too well that when we ask for glory or recognition, it is often because we have felt so badly about ourselves that we were hoping for relief. We may even have tried to fool ourselves by some mental trick. We may have said, "If I win the lottery, I will give to the church and do good with the money." We may have said the same thing about parole or shock probation or a new trial. That is called bargaining; we often do it while we are grieving loss or when we feel sad.

Unfortunately, our bargaining is mostly about our own sadness. It's really about not feeling, sensing or knowing how important we already are. One of the reasons people struggle so much with this false pride is that they aren't letting themselves know how important they are in God's eyes. They believe the world's values but God's values and the world's values have almost nothing in common. Let's admit that when we have struggled the most with false pride, it was when we felt the worst and measured ourselves by the world's yardstick rather than by God's. When we really know that God loves us and that individually we are important to the God of the universe, it is easier to be humble, to give up bargaining, to care about others and to reach out to them

Jesus was praying for us even though he knew he soon would die. He died so that we could be in his family and be freed from sin any time we got stuck in it. Jewish tradition teaches about reaching for glory in a similar way. It says that during every generation there are at least seven faithful people who go quietly about their daily tasks, receiving little or no recognition from the world. Yet because of their faith and goodness, the world survives. It is often these kinds of people in the community who receive little or no applause or recognition who are the most important. They are the saints who, by their goodness, protect all of the rest of us. Their kindness touches us and inspires us. Their generosity encourages us to be generous. Their compassion, kindness and honesty often cause us to re-examine ourselves and to require more of ourselves. Some of you are like that. Some of you quietly reach out to people who are hurting. You have put your faith into action.

Jesus' attitude in this passage can teach us so much. One implied theme is the trust Jesus demonstrated that he had in God and in God's choices for him. His attitude seems to be, "If God is doing it, or has ordained it, it must be good." His attitude of adoration and thanksgiving toward God seems to be about a conviction that God only wants good for us. There are many people around me and around you who quietly evidence God's goodness and the power of faith in their lives. They are living, breathing examples of faith put into action. They show how God can use even tragedy, pain and sorrow for good, even when evil may have caused these tribulations.

All sin has something in common. All sin distrusts God and disbelieves in God's ultimate care for us. You remember the story of Eve and the serpent. The serpent tricked Eve by getting her to believe that God would withhold something good from her and that she had to take things into her own hands to get what she deserved. That is the way that all sin tempts us. Sin tries to trick us into disbelieving that God wants the very best for us and into believing that what we can do for ourselves is better than waiting for what God will do for us.

The story is told about a man who deeply wanted to know the difference between heaven and hell. He prayed for wisdom and understanding about the difference. In a dream, an angel took him to both places. First, he was taken to hell, where elaborate tables of food were prepared, and yet the people were all starving. The man noticed that even though there was food in abundance, everyone's elbows were stiff and they couldn't feed themselves. Next, he was taken to heaven and there, to his amazement, were the same tables filled with food. And there, everyone was healthy and happy. The man noticed that the people in heaven also had stiff elbows. They couldn't feed themselves either.

He asked the angel, "How are all these people so happy and content?" The angel told him. "Here in heaven," the angel said, "everyone feeds each other."

When we pray, are we mainly praying for what we want or for what God wants? Are we looking for evidence that we are right or evidence that God is right? Are you willing to look for examples of the kindness and goodness of others instead of focusing on your own goodness and kindness?

It is my prayer that each of us will let God's love for us into our lives so much that we will be transformed every day into knowing and sensing God's love and value for us. I pray that we will feel this so powerfully that we will be even more protected from sin, and that others can be inspired by our faith. Amen.

. . . the Holy Spirit will teach all things.

In the same way that there are a variety of gifts of the Spirit spoken of in 1 Corinthians 12: 4, there are also a variety of churches. They emphasize different gifts: some speak in tongues, some demonstrate excellent teaching, some prophesy. These different styles can overwhelm us sometimes. How do we know what's right and good? How can we know what is from God - or coming from within ourselves or from others? The churches don't even agree on what's important—or do they?

Philippians 2: 12-13 tells us " . . . work out your own salvation with fear and trembling; for it is God who is at work in you, enabling you both to will and to work for his good pleasure." Most churches agree on the important things. Also, though, each of us is responsible for the choices we make. As we come to understand Scripture and then begin to apply it, we can each be even more responsible. We can move toward the essence of Truth, and then no one can simply blame a particular church and say, "Oh, they steered me wrong." In Revelation, God tells the seven churches seven different things! However, no message has to do with how the Spirit lives in that church. The Holy Spirit is always the Holy Spirit.

God is really only interested in whether or not we sin. Period. Church style is a matter of choice and taste. What we really have as our guide is Scripture. Every day, Scripture has something to teach us if we will listen. We must be cautious, though, for at times, evil will also try to use Scripture. Evil tries to trick us into losing our blessings. It seeks our very lives and souls. Evil used the interpretation of Scripture to trick Eve and it attempted to trick Jesus. So how can we know whether the voice speaking to us is from good or evil? The answer is that evil's use of Scripture looks true only on one level. The tree's fruit looked good but God had commanded Adam and Eve not to eat of it. Evil challenged God's Word and defied Scripture on another level. When the Holy Spirit teaches, it is true on all levels, and all agree with Scripture, with God's Word.

The term *Holy Spirit* means "comforter" and "confronter." The term *Satan* means "accuser of the brethren." If the chastisement you hear is about something you did a long time ago that you've already confessed, it's safe to believe that thought is coming from evil. Evil uses those old sins to demoralize us today. Evil will say things like, "See what kind of person you are for having done that." Sometimes evil may attempt to evoke guilt about something you've already confessed to and have stopped doing. This kind of guilt leads to destruction. Guilt and shame can be so overwhelming as to break a person's spirit.

139

The Holy Spirit, though, will confront us and point out our sin, either as we think about it, commit it or in the aftermath—but only until we repent and confess. The Holy Spirit's purpose is to get us to avoid sin or to stop sinning, and to confess sin so that we can be made clean—not so that we will feel badly about ourselves. The Holy Spirit's purpose is to lead us to repentance. What God has forgiven is over for God. God wants to lift you up and evil wants to tear you down

The Holy Spirit will teach us all things. Let's face it, though, all of us have learning problems in one way or another. The Holy Spirit has had a tough time teaching us to stop certain sins that we have relied upon for support. The Holy Spirit will teach you all things. Is it possible that we could use our faith to help us learn things that lead to a G.E.D.? If we look, the Holy Spirit is teaching when people are learning janitorial skills as well as when others are learning horticulture, maintenance, business skills or basic math. The Holy Spirit will also teach you all things that the Bible teaches. The Bible is God's Word to us. The Holy Spirit will be in line with Scripture and will be teaching us morality.

The image of the righteous person in Proverbs is one willing and eager to learn. Some lessons are harder for us to learn than others. And some may be much easier. Yet our attitude of willingness to learn is in part coming from the Holy Spirit. The fool is someone who says, "I know now all I need to know." Some people refuse to learn because they want to preserve their sin. Sometimes the Holy Spirit teaches us through Scripture and sometimes through special people - ministers, teachers, evangelists, peers and our families. Sometimes the Holy Spirit speaks through our children. How humbling it is to see a child picking up our bad language, for example.

The Holy Spirit will also remind us of all that Jesus said to us. Just like the disciples, the Holy Spirit will encourage us and bring us together in one mind. The more we are willing to learn Scripture, the more the Holy Spirit will bring it to mind.

Would you commit yourself to learning at least two verses this week? Would you commit yourself to learning and putting to permanent memory two more verses from the Bible this week? Are you willing for the Holy Spirit to teach you, even if it isn't teaching what you want? Would you be willing right now to commit to God that you want to learn by asking God to come into your heart and teach you what to learn and to direct your path?

It is my prayer that each of us would more fully be able to learn, so we can remember and can witness for God in our daily actions. Amen.

71

Receiving Abundant Mercy
                    Isa 55: 6-11, Phil 1: 21-27, Mt 20: 1-16

The best time to look for people is when they can be found.

"Seek ye the Lord while he may be found." When that phrase is out of the
context of the chapter, it could almost sound harsh. When you read the
rest of the chapter before it, you realize God is inviting His children to
come close so they can be blessed. "Ho, everyone who thirsts, come to
the waters; and you who have no money come, buy and eat! Come buy
wine and milk without money and without price." (Isaiah 55:1)

We are told to seek the Lord while He invites those He loves near. How
can that be? We know that God is always present. Why are we invited
near "while He may be found?" This is a beautifully poetic way of saying
there are times when our sin and fear interfere with our ability to sense
God's presence. There are times when we feel that we cannot be close to
God, times when we feel especially lonely. There are times when we feel
as if our prayers are not heard. I have heard this described by some as a
feeling that prayers haven't gotten any farther than the ceiling. But God
doesn't move during these times. Only our ability to perceive God moves.
God is telling us here to take advantage of the chances and opportunities
we do have to get closer to Him. We do this through repentance. Most of
us have on-going things of which we can repent. When we do this, we
move closer to our God, who is always there.

We are told to "let the wicked forsake their way and the unrighteous their
thoughts." The word *wicked* conjures up images of people working hard to
be bad. The word really refers to people who have gotten so wrapped up
in the things of the world that they have forgotten God. This verse speaks
to people who have gotten so caught up in schoolwork, business, legal
work, hobbies, cliques, friends and other things that they have forgotten
God. How do people forget God? By just never paying much attention, by
not intentionally spending time in prayer, study or services.

Who among us has not been guilty of neglecting or forgetting God
because we were so busy, involved and preoccupied? The word
"unrighteous" here refers to people who don't disbelieve. They just don't
commit to being believers. They may pray out of habit. They probably
think of themselves as good people. But they have ignored what they
know God requires of them. Doing what God asks, expects or requires just
isn't in their plan. No, they aren't openly against God; they simply don't
pay Him much more than lip service. They ignore God and God's Word.
Jesus said that there was more hope for the person who disbelieves than
for these folks.

God tells us that He will have abundant mercy on the person who repents. Who among us does not need to repent? Who among us spends as much time with God and God's Word as He desires for us? Who among us allows the words to have the effect they should? Sure, we may read and we may pray but are we taking God's Word seriously? Do you not have things of which you need to repent? Repentance is our open acknowledgement that we have been resisting God's thoughts, and that we are willing to accept them over our own. God is calling the wicked and the unrighteous because He knows they are missing out on the blessings and the opportunities.

In the next verse, God tells us, "For my thoughts are not your thoughts, nor are your ways my ways." In our sinful arrogance, we act as if we can judge God's actions and His Words. At times, we have disagreed with things God says to do or not to do. We have judged them, calling them old-fashioned, ancient, silly or unfair. We have rejected the rules that we didn't want to follow. Wrapping ourselves in self-righteousness, we can trick ourselves into believing that some token response would be enough. Would it be enough if you tipped someone a quarter for saving your life?

"For as the heavens are higher than the earth, so are my ways higher than your ways." To get a little better picture of the truth of what God is saying, imagine a grain of salt in your hand. Imagine that that grain of salt represents you and everyone that you know. Now imagine that the entire Earth represents the universe in similar relation to that tiny grain of salt to you. You may begin to get a vague idea of how huge is the universe! When we judge the Creator of the universe by our standards, it is almost comical. And yet, most of us have done it and probably will again. God knows this and isn't offended–especially when we are willing to begin looking for what He says makes sense instead of wanting to use our own rules.

God tells us that His Word goes forth from His mouth and it shall not return empty. It shall accomplish that which He proposes, and prosper in the thing for which He sent it. His Word is so powerful and active—living and active, according to Hebrews. So what can we do? We can acknowledge and accept that God's thoughts are higher than our own. We can go ahead and repent of the attitudes and ways of thinking that condemned and ignored God. We can repent our sins.

It is my prayer that we begin to trust in God and His Word and that we begin to really rest in the confidence of being able to depend on Him and His Word for answers, guidance, comfort and inspiration. Further, it is my prayer that each of us becomes the salt God has called on us to be. Amen.

72

You Can Find Peace
Prov 8: 22-31, Jn 20: 19-23, 1 Pet 1: 1-9

Wisdom is a gift to all who want to be closer to God.

In these verses, Wisdom is recounting her achievements. She has a long list of her accomplishments to her credit! As we read this passage, some of us may be reminded of feelings we have when we meet a very successful person, someone like Wisdom who has many accomplishments under her belt. You know the type. Just being in their presence can leave us feeling inadequate! Some of us feel inspired when we meet someone like this but some of us get drained of hope. When we see their talent, beauty, intelligence - whatever - we feel fumbled-fingered, ugly and slow. Yet sometimes when you see someone who has talent, ability or accomplishment, you can feel the hope of achievement beating faster. In part, wisdom can be that for us if we allow it to be. Through faith, we can have more of this feeling.

When the talent, ability and beauty of others seem to drain us of hope because they seem so unlike us, part of the problem is our attitude of self-criticism. You know, when someone is locked into seeing and hearing criticism, it almost doesn't matter what you say because the person will hear and feel criticized. Very few weeks in the prison went by that people I complimented didn't feel insulted because of what they thought I said. They were ready to hear criticism and so they did. It was automatic - they heard what they feared. When folks are in that place of being scared of old hurts, it is easy to remember the things that caused them to feel ashamed. We have all been there in the land of self-criticism. We try to motivate ourselves by being even tougher on ourselves. The problem is that motivation through fear or belittling never works.

There may have been times we have ignored our failures because they seemed so overwhelming. Sometimes we have denied our failures or sin so often we didn't know the truth from dishonesty. In the middle of an attitude of "poor me," the only goal we've had is to defend ourselves from even more insults to our self-esteem, pride or hope. In this state, feeling so down and defeated, or so far behind that catching up felt impossible, it was very difficult to resist temptation.

Imagine having the ability to do what you really want. Think of the thing that has really eluded you. Think of what you haven't been able to do in the past. Perhaps it would be to resist a certain temptation. Perhaps it is to calm your anger. Maybe you have always wanted to feel good about yourself. Take a moment now and imagine that you can see yourself being able to overcome this. Close your eyes if you like. Then, as you open them, you can feel a sense of accomplishment and strength. Take a deep breath and simply feel the sensations of what it would be like to have the ability to accomplish that. If you were able to sense that accomplishment, you just saw the future, because wisdom can give you that ability. Through wisdom we can change, grow, get healthier, happier and become more capable of doing whatever is good.

Throughout the Bible, wisdom is given as a gift so people can do righteous acts. In the Book of Exodus, God gives wisdom in the form of talent and ability. Wisdom is portrayed as being visible in certain talents, learned abilities and crafts. In other parts of Proverbs, wisdom is seen as wise understanding and a willingness to follow God's law. For example, a few that I especially like are: Proverbs 1:7, "The fear of the Lord is the beginning of knowledge; fools despise wisdom and instruction;" Proverbs 2: 10-11, "For wisdom will come into your heart, and knowledge will be pleasant to your soul, prudence will watch over you and understanding will guard you;" Proverbs 12:8, "One is commended for good sense, but a perverse mind is despised;" and Proverbs 15: 21, "Folly is joy to one who has no sense, but a person of understanding walks straight ahead."

Real wisdom is being able to agree with God even though sometimes our feelings tell us something else. For example, you know that in God's eyes if you have confessed your sin and want to do better, you are forgiven. Yet you may not feel forgiven or you may not forgive yourself. Wisdom is agreeing with God even if we don't feel forgiven. It is the same with feeling worthy. We may not feel worthy of God caring about us or even believing that other human beings can love us. But we trust that in God's eyes we have value. Part of real wisdom is seeing life as God sees it.

The more you put God's Words into your heart and spirit, the more wisdom you will have to call on for strength. The more you have God's Words in your mind, the more God's wisdom will be expressed in your thoughts and in your actions. The more you take God's Words into your heart, mind and spirit, the more you will begin to notice changes in yourself you did not think possible. You can like yourself, a person others trust and like, and someone that others look to for wisdom and guidance. Are you ready to accept God's wisdom into your heart, mind and spirit? Ask and it shall be given unto you. Seek and ye shall find. Knock and it shall be opened to you. God be praised, you are already on the path. You are already on the journey.

It is my prayer that each of us would more fully feel God's acceptance of us and His joy in our success. I especially pray that each of us sense God's joy as we succeed in our goals, and as we enjoy the blessings that He has given to us and wants to give us in the future. Amen.

To be faithful means to be continually making adjustments.

"Come, let us return to the Lord . . ." What wonderful encouragement! How appropriate, too, for we always need to return to the Lord. Even those of us who think we are superior spiritually need to return to God. Perhaps those times when we have been arrogant and feeling very self-righteous are the times we need to return to the Lord the most.

Sin and the need for repentance are with all of us. To be faithful is to be continually making adjustments, to be correcting, and realigning with God's Word. Some of the time we recognize our need to readjust our behavior, and some of time God sends us words and experiences which tell us to change. Sometimes we receive words by getting warnings or write-ups, and sometimes words come in a loving fashion through a friend. There are at least a thousand ways through which God can tell us that it is time to change. Sometimes we know inside that we have left the Lord. Sometimes we only recognize it when someone or something points it out to us.

" . . . for it is he who has torn, and he will heal us." It often hurts to recognize that we have been wrong even when a friend tells us. It feels as if we are being torn or ripped apart. Let's admit it together. It is unpleasant to discover that we need to change. We want to have gotten beyond needing to make corrections. It is easy for us to fall into thinking that we are right or that we always have the correct answers. At least that is the way our pride usually treats the knowledge.

Sometimes God speaks loudly because we have not been listening to the whispers, hints and direct challenges to our actions as written in the Bible. When we have been ignoring God's warning by reassuring ourselves rather than examining ourselves, we can indeed seem as though we are being torn or ripped apart. But sometimes it takes a good ripping to get us out of our ruts! In effect, all sin has consequences. We can let the consequences remind us to return to God or we can ignore them. The world will try to blame the consequences on someone who is out to get us. The world may attempt to say that the consequences of sin rarely occur and may call all consequences "accidents." How deceitful. When God corrects us, it isn't an accident on His part. When we are being faithful, we change our behavior and thank God for protecting us from going the wrong way

" . . . for it is he who has torn, and he will heal us." The consequences of sin or punishment from God are never for meanness. God's punishments are always to heal us of our greater illness, an illness that is separating us from the truth. Once we are over the initial hurt, we can appreciate that God stopped us. Have you ever noticed the difference between how faithful people talk and how people talk who still need to return to the Lord? People still caught up in crime and sin say, "I caught a charge," as if charges were caught like the common cold. People still caught up in crime do not want to admit that their actions brought about the arrest warrant. People still sinning may not want to take an honest look at their sin.

Those who are returning to the Lord often thank God for having been arrested or held accountable because they know they were prevented from continuing their crimes or other sins. The sinful life was "arrested" and they were given the opportunity to heal. A sign on a church bulletin board said, "Anger often gets us into trouble. Pride keeps us there." Anger, greed, envy, lust or fear may prompt us into sin. It is often pride that keeps us there. Pride doesn't want us to examine ourselves.

Hosea reassures us that we will be restored. "On the third day he will raise us up." Let us know the Lord. His going forth is as sure as the dawn. We can have reassurance every morning. Many people thank God in prayer for waking up. It is a reassurance. Recognizing the blessing of waking is a way of being faithful. We can count on God restoring us, accepting us and then re-accepting us. In the midst of accepting our sin, it is good to receive reassurance that God cares about us. It helps to know that God is as dependable as the dawn. We will be restored if we are willing to repent. Repentance is a sign that we accept God's love for us. Repentance is our acknowledgement that God was right and our actions were wrong. Repentance is a way of saying thanks for correcting and keeping us from further harm.

Our feelings follow from what we tell ourselves and believe but they also come from what we want. When folks revert to following their feelings they have rejected God and have made an altar of certain feelings. If our repentance is genuine, it will withstand all temptations. When faithful people have repented, lapses into sin are met with almost immediate remorse and desire for healing and restoration. Real repentance means we know that what we did was wrong. Even though we may still have the urge, we want to be beyond it. We become very committed to change.

It is my prayer that our repentance is and will be sincere no matter which emotions we encounter. I especially pray that each of us will hear God's love for us in His correction of us. Amen.

What we store in our hearts and souls says a lot about our faith.

These words say that God loves us. He has done many things for us and for the faithful who came before us. One of the important things God has given us is the Commandments. Indirectly, they also are referred to here. It is good for us to store up the Commandments and directives God has given us. Why? It's because the rules were designed for us and created for our benefit.

God's law teaches us what righteousness is and gives us direction. It's more, though. When you give your child directions, it is in part to keep the child safe. You tell your children and other loved young ones things that express your love for them: Look both ways before crossing the street, be careful, stay away from strangers. Parents who really love their children want them to pay attention to their words because they are protective. We're told to keep God's Words in our hearts and souls, in the deepest recesses of ourselves. This is protective. When we store God's Words in our hearts and souls, they become a part of our core being.

A number of years ago, a woman I knew developed Alzheimer's disease. When I visited her, about every five minutes she would ask," What did you say your name was?" even though she knew me well. I would tell her and it was clear that she might forget in five minutes. Still, she knew and loved the Lord. She could sing many, many hymns. At her core, she loved God. When everything else was stripped away, she still had God in her life. That was a powerful testimony to her faith. There wasn't any pretense or fear covering up who she really was. God's Words were stored deep in her heart and were lifted up in song.

We're told in Deuteronomy 26, "See, I am setting before you today a blessing and a curse." We have to choose. Do you want God's blessings or just the world's? Do you want God's blessings or just what you can get yourself? There are many ways we can respond to the love of God. Certainly we get blessed the more we follow God's directives in our lives. Reading God's Words every day is to put them deep into our souls. It is also to put them as a sign in our hands, ready for instant access. People who are serious about change know that change begins with our minds, with what we think. It also includes our emotions and attitudes. We change both by what we dwell on and by the emotions we allow to play in our hearts.

The Book of Philippians tells us to dwell on whatever is true, honorable, just, pure, lovely, and gracious. We are to dwell on anything worthy of praise or excellence. Nothing comes closer to all that than the Bible. I have a friend who meditates on Scripture throughout the day. He takes a verse and dwells on it while he works and does various things. It helps him to put God's Word deep into his soul. He would tell you he has received many blessings as a result.

Recently a young woman told me she prays throughout the day as she goes about her business. She said she feels God's peace through her being alone with God in prayer. I told her that I often do a similar thing. I pray often throughout the day. Another friend gave me this prayer: "So far today God, I've done all right. I haven't gossiped. I haven't lost my temper. I haven't been grumpy, nasty or selfish. I'm really glad for that. But in a few minutes, God, I'm going to get out of bed. I'm going to need a lot of help after that." Most of us know that we also need help.

If we look at any trouble we have now or had in the past, sin is and was a part of that problem. Sin is a part of any problem or real difficulty we have. Often it is the sin of pride that causes us to refuse to recognize that our problems are the direct result of sin. Most of us would rather not see sin in our problems because we would then feel even guiltier, bad or unworthy. Yet God's message to us is that we are loved and that our righteousness does not depend on whether we can keep a perfectly clean slate. It depends on our putting faith in God's ability. The friend I told you about earlier who meditates on God's Word says that when he notices sin or temptation, he tells God that he can't defeat the enemy but he knows that God can. He relies on his faith to help him. He refuses to argue with temptation. He simply gives it to God.

The more we store up God's Words in our hearts and minds, the more they come out in ways we could not have foreseen. In fact, if we take Hebrews literally, the Word of God is alive and contains God's Spirit. When we take it inside ourselves, it heals and protects us from the inside out. We are told to do this so our days will be multiplied and also so we can experience a little bit of Heaven upon Earth.

Once while talking with my son about faith, the Bible and God, I got to feel even closer him and to God. I got to have a very intimate talk with my son and feel his love both for me and for God. That is a little bit of Heaven. The truth is that every time we really allow ourselves to feel God loving us and share that with our loved ones, we can feel closer still. We can also feel that closeness with others when we share those golden moments of revelation given to us. We all receive encouragement from each other.

It is my prayer that we become so filled with God's Words that His love even for our enemies comes streaming out of our actions, thoughts and talk. Amen.

We can speak with humble hearts.

Today's passage is one that is considered to be one of the great prophetic passages, allowing us to take a real look at the heart of a prophet. It captures the emotion that many of us feel toward God when we let ourselves be close!

Jeremiah is talking to God. Jeremiah had suffered a great deal. You might think that he would complain about the abuse, humiliation or verbal slurs he had experienced. You might think he would be saying, "God, You have deceived me. I thought that by being a worker for you, I would be safe." Isn't this what many of us have thought, that if we were righteous enough, we'd be protected from bad things occurring in our lives? Many of us also have believed that being righteous would protect our families from disaster. But while being righteous does protect us from some things, it doesn't protect us from pain and suffering. Job tells us that pain and suffering fall on the just as well as the unjust. This can be a difficult thing to accept. It can also lead to a deepening of faith.

Jeremiah certainly could have complained to God about all the abuse he had experienced. But here he was, complaining to God that he felt deceived because he had no idea that his compulsion to tell others what God had told him would be so strong! Jeremiah said that when he tried to shut these feelings up inside of himself, it felt like burning fire in his chest. That reminds me of the words of the disciples on the road to Emmaus, "Were not our hearts burning with us?" When we come to know God in the midst of chaos and crisis, we can feel a compulsion to share our spiritual insight with someone else. The peace and comfort we have received . . . well, we just feel that we must tell someone about it.

I was at my father's bedside the night he was dying in the hospital. I spent time reading the Bible waiting for the sad and inevitable to happen. Suddenly, a peace and an assurance that everything would be all right came over me. It was so powerful and so good that remembering it revives my enthusiasm. It helps remind me of that type of deep satisfaction and comfort we can receive when there is a tragedy occurring. Afterward, I wanted to know about other people who had also felt that peace and comfort in the face of death. And I wanted to share my experience with others.

Pain and suffering come into every life. For some, the difficulties can mount up until they seem overwhelming. I can't tell you why some people—very kind and good people—can seem more afflicted with tragedy and difficulty. Still, some of the most deeply spiritual people I know are folks who have been through very, very tough times. Their faith makes a difference in their lives. Because of it, they are not bitter. They get irritable at times like the rest of us, but their faith beams out at anyone willing to see it.

I remember a woman I knew at the Kentucky Correctional Institute for Women who seemed perpetually happy. Some people thought her happiness and enthusiasm were false but it never seemed fake to me. I believed she was genuinely joyful. She had found the Lord, and you could just tell by being around her that she had discovered a deep inner peace and happiness. On the surface, in a worldly view, she didn't have much to rejoice about. She had had a difficult life. But in a spiritual way, she had a life of plenty. And if you let her, she would tell you about how good God had been to her.

I know that you also may have been deeply touched by God. You may know that God has delivered you from much in your life. Perhaps like Jeremiah, you have been delivered from death. Or perhaps you have been delivered from foolish mistakes and stubbornness. And now you may feel that you want to tell others about your journey. When we let God into our hearts and we really start receiving the blessings he has to offer us, we want to share it with someone. We can tell others in a respectful and humble way. This kind of one-to-one witnessing can be very powerful.

The Reverend Billy Graham tells of witnessing this kind of one-to-one sharing and of how it led him to God. Without this spiritual sharing, he might never have pursued his ministry. Of course, God has particular opportunities just for you. There are people who come into your life who can be touched and blessed just by watching how you conduct your life of faith. Sometimes, no words are necessary. As we mature spiritually, we no longer care if we get any recognition. We know that God sees and that is good enough. Recently, a mother was telling me about her daughter, who had been using drugs and getting into trouble. Then, with her mother's help, the daughter turned her life around. With tears in her eyes, the mother told me of her deep gratitude that God had touched her daughter's heart. Even though that mother had been much of the conduit of God's love for that young woman, the mother wanted no praise. She was just so happy, pleased and relieved because her daughter was clean and sober. Her story was about God, not about herself.

It is my prayer that each of us be able to feel that fire burning in our hearts that lets us know we are in the presence of the Lord. I especially pray that each of us would start sensing God's presence so powerfully in our lives that we will be able to let God bring us even more cleansing and healing. Amen.

Giving Kindness
2 Kings 4:8-16, Rom 6:1-11, Mt 10:37-42

What more powerful connection is there than a connection through faith?

Although we do not know who this wealthy woman was who lived in Shunem, we do know that God blessed her through the prophet Elisha. If you read the passage right before this one, you see that Elisha had just richly blessed a very poor woman in a different town, so we know he was not showing favoritism because of the Shunammite woman's wealth. We also know that this wealthy Shunammite woman wanted to help Elisha, not just because he was in need, but also because he represented God. In verse 9 she said to her husband, "Look, I am sure that this man who regularly passes our way is a man of God. Let us make a small roof chamber with walls, and put there for him a bed, a table, a chair, and a lamp, so that he can stay there whenever he comes to us."

This woman wanted to make Elisha a permanent place to stay when he was traveling in their city. She wanted to do something for God through doing something for Elisha. This is because she recognized him as a man of God. As the book Titus says, "To the pure, all things are pure." The purity of this woman's faith was able to see Elisha's purity. When we are in touch with God, we can recognize other people who are also.

When we help someone who is a believer or a minister, it is different than when we help a non-believer. When we help non-believers, that help is a type of evangelism. We are extending kindness, in part, because we are believers. We would like for the nonbeliever to become a believer. It's different when we help a minister or a believer. Jesus said doing so would bring us a special reward (Matthew 10:41). He or she that receives a prophet in the name of a prophet shall receive a prophet's reward, and he or she that receives a righteous person in the name of a righteous person shall receive a righteous person's reward.

It sounds as if the way to be especially blessed is to help righteous people. There are special blessings also for helping those people who can't help themselves. Here—and plainly in Matthew—helping even with a drink of water for those who belong to Christ, because they belong to Christ, will be rewarded.

In reflecting on this passage, it makes sense that God blesses us especially when we do good things for righteous people. In part, it is a statement of faith. It is an act of belief in God and a desire to do for those close to God. We are acting on the belief that we are family and that we feel a bond, a real connection. What more powerful connection is there than one through faith?

I like to do for believers. It's a way to return the thanks and appreciation I feel for my having been blessed. I want others to be blessed, too. Do you find yourself wanting to help other righteous folks? Some folks have said they especially enjoy helping believers because they feel close to them. When helping non-believers, you can have that hope of becoming close.

After receiving the kindness of the rich woman, Elisha and Gehazi wanted to do for her. They wanted to return kindness where it had been shown to them. Like Elisha and Gehazi, we want to do for those people who have done for us. It is a way of binding us closer together as a community and as believers. We tend to feel close to the people who have extended an honest kindness to us. We get to feel good doing for others. Elisha and Gehazi were no different. They wanted to do something that would richly bless the Shunammite woman. When they realized she was old and childless, they knew how to bless her. God must have told them something about this, because to pronounce what God is going to do specifically for a person is arrogant. Elisha and Gehazi gave to the woman what she wanted most, even though she didn't ask for it. It seems that we get richly blessed for small acts of kindness carried out through a belief in God.

People who commit selfless acts of kindness for others have had some tremendous blessings occur in their lives. I am sure you have seen some amazing things this way. I have seen people make parole, even being called up early, when they themselves didn't see any possibility of it. I have seen people receive health and opportunities–seemingly miraculous events. They received blessings and could then bless others.

If we do for others just to get a blessing, we only get that blessing. If we do for others because we want to serve the Lord, and because we want to be a part of God's wonderful plan to reach out and bless believers, we will be blessed in ways we could never have foreseen. Our God is a good God. You won't out give Him! If we begin to really be kind, we would begin to change ourselves. That sends a powerful message!

If you want to be a part of that message, do something this week for some believers just because they are believers. Be especially kind, and if you have those old judgmental thoughts, pray about your tendency to judge. Ask God to extend your ability to offer kindness.

It is my prayer that we recognize that all the kindness and sacrifice that has been extended to us as believers since ancient times. I also pray that each of us will allow ourselves to feel that kindness as an encouragement to do even more than we are doing. Amen.

In Him, we are free indeed.

This passage begins with the words, "Rejoice greatly daughter Zion . . ." Truly this is deep wisdom, posed in simplicity and poetic phrasing. We are encouraged and instructed—as in so many places in the Bible—to worship, rejoice, praise, give thanks, and use our voice and our hands to make a joyful noise. When we do these things, we are richly blessed. That is the way we were created. The more we give thanks and praise God, the better we will feel. The more time we spend thanking God, the stronger, more content and more secure we feel, whether we are alone or with others.

Many giants of faith have done exactly this. Mother Theresa recommended that everyone spend 30 minutes in the morning and in the evening praising God and rejoicing. She credited her ability to accomplish as much as she did to her time spent this way. She believed that it deepened faith. (Mother Theresa also said if you don't have time for these 30 minutes morning and evening, you ought to spend 60!) Praising God sets our attitude and brings us closer to Him.

Not too long ago a woman I know told me how she began spending time praising God. She was the happiest with herself that I had ever seen her. I thank God that she and others have discovered and are discovering how blessed we can become when we use this simple technique to begin and end each day. I take time for praise and rejoicing when I first awaken, while I exercise, while I'm driving, or while I am eating breakfast. Sometimes I do it while appreciating how fortunate I am to be able to worship with people, including you.

The rest of the verse reads, "Lo, your King comes to you; triumphant and victorious is he, humble and riding on a donkey, on a colt, the foal of a donkey." The King comes to us humble and in a spiritual way. All that is required to see Him is to look for the spiritual part of life. The Hebrew word translated as *victorious* means "able to save," the power to have moral victory.

Jesus criticized the people of his day who dismissed John the Baptist because he didn't dress in fine flowing robes. John the Baptist wore what in today's world would look like the clothes of a homeless person. Many people may never recognize some of the most deeply spiritual people because they do not have (and may never have) limousines, big salaries or fame. They go quietly about what they do during the day in one giant prayer - sometimes praising God, sometimes waiting for God to speak to them, sometimes just enjoying what they are doing and doing it as well as they can because they are doing it for the glory of God.

The deeply spiritual people know it is not important that the world credits what they do; it is what they do for God that brings satisfaction. We can all have that satisfaction whether we are sweeping floors, building buildings or cleaning out bedpans. It is an attitude.

In this passage, we're told that God will cut off the chariot from Ephraim and the warhorse from Jerusalem. In other words, He will give us peace. He will take from us the desire to war and fight. People who love the Lord often find that their anger and temper begin to cool. Many people have noticed that the closer to the Lord they come, the more they want to be kind to others. Self-control is one of the fruits of the Spirit mentioned in Galatians. You remember: we get love, joy, peace, patience, kindness, generosity, faithfulness, gentleness and self-control. These are the gifts of the Spirit, the blessings we receive as we move closer to God.

This passage has even more wisdom. Verse 11 states that as daughters of Zion and because of God's covenant with you, He will set your captives free. What encouragement! We will all be set free no matter what miserable pit of despair we have been in. He will free us from the addiction of sin. He will make us free of despair. He will set us free from whatever seems to bind us and prevents us from being free. For some of us, it may be loneliness; for others, the shame of the past; for still others, perhaps jealousy, rage or fear. He will set us free from our grief and sadness. Real freedom comes from drawing close to God. In Him, we are free indeed.

"Return to your stronghold; O prisoners of hope; today I declare that I will restore to you double." What a wonderful phrase: prisoners of hope! For me, it is the opposite of being caught in the grip of despair. When we live with hope, it seems to energize us. Hope encourages us and gives us reason to look forward. It lessens our hurt, brightens our days, and calms our fears. Hope protects us from despair. It keeps us from giving up. It inspires us to work even harder and to hold on longer.

When we praise God, we are blessed in important ways. It may be in the way in which God often respects our past by not doing away with it but by transforming it. Fishermen become fishers of men. People prone to war are made first into people who depend on God and have peace, and who then can become warriors for the Lord.

It is my prayer that as you rejoice, you will allow God more deeply into your heart and mind. I also pray that you let God's gifts sustain you and bless you. Amen.

Prayer Is Healing
Isa 66: 18-23, Heb 12: 7-13, Lk 13: 22-30

Good traits like patience and confidence grow from good thoughts.

One thing that is clear from this passage: God sees a big difference between arrogance and humility. There are distinctions made like this throughout the Bible. There is the sorting out of the sheep from the goats, the wheat from the tares, the quick from the dead, the saved from the lost, and the faithful from the unfaithful. There are people whom God loves and people in whose prayer He delights. There are prayers He refuses. It has become popular to think of God as all loving and forgiving but this is only half of the story.

Throughout the Bible, God's position on sin is clear: He hates it and punishes it. God especially punishes people who refuse to become repentant about their sin. God is seen as especially angry with people who refuse to acknowledge His right to declare what is sinful and what is not. God punishes rebellion and rewards repentance. We are encouraged to seek out God's blessings and to avoid His wrath. From Genesis through Revelation, God respects honesty and humility, and rewards people who listen to His Words and follow His commands.

We read, "For I know their words and their thoughts . . ." It is scary to think that God knows our thoughts! It is bad enough that God knows those things we have done when no one else was looking but God even knows all the thoughts we have had—even those about sin and about Him. We can dislike the fact that God knows our thoughts. We could even call it an invasion of privacy.

Yet a position of faith might ask, "Why is God interested in what I think?" If God wants know what we think then what we allow ourselves to think about must be as important as what we do. And it is. Our thoughts are important to God because God is aware of how our thoughts affect our future, and how they make sense of our past and present. How we think determines who we are and who we are going to be. Our thoughts precede our actions. There is no such thing as, "I didn't think." We may not have thought what happened would happen, but we did think. Sometimes we thought about and wanted something to occur long before it happened. Today's anger and desire for revenge may very much be driving something that will happen tomorrow. We might call what happens an accident, but really it would have been the result of reckless thoughts. When we harbor unclean thoughts in our minds, our futures get dirty as well. The thoughts we think, what we dwell on, what we allow ourselves to savor and really desire in our minds do affect us in very powerful ways.

Proverbs 23:7 says, "For as he thinketh in his heart, so is he." Jesus said it this way: "What comes out of a person is what defiles a person, from within out of the heart of a person come evil thoughts, fornication, theft, murder, adultery, coveting, wickedness, deceit, licentiousness, envy, slander, pride and foolishness." Knowing our thoughts, God can steer us to prosperity, a word that in the Bible is about much more than money. The word is translated from the Hebrew word *shalom*—peace and abundance of health, happiness and right relationships of peace among us, and between God and us.

We have all had thoughts we knew were wrong. Yet we can decide to do as Jesus said, "Seek ye first the kingdom of heaven." We can decide to become serious about our faith and our lives by changing at the source. When we change our thinking, we change our lives. Romans 12:2 tells us, " . . . be transformed by the renewing of your minds . . ." Be changed, renewed, born again, resurrected and cleansed. Get a new start, a new beginning by changing what you think and what you think about. So how do we do that? "How do I change my thoughts?" you ask.

Each of us must decide individually from where our truth will come. Where can you go for advice, direction and guidance for your life? Our logic is faulty; our eyes can be deceived as easily as our ears and hearts can be. Joshua 24: 15 says, "Choose you this day whom you will serve . . . but as for me and my household, we will serve the Lord."

When you find yourself worrying, or becoming angry or sad or afraid, let your mind begin to dwell on God. You may want to start with prayer or you may want to recall some passage of Scripture or truth that God has given to you. Perhaps you may want to recall some of the beautiful things of the world God created, like trees, grass, flowers, stones or the sky. These are ways to begin, and to get relief and to begin experiencing peace and prosperity. With the psalmist you can say," I lift up my eyes to the hills. From whence does my help come? My help comes from the Lord, who made heaven and earth. He will not let your foot be moved." When you agree with God, you allow your mind to be transformed.

It is my prayer that each of us will be able to sense deeply God's Spirit with us in times of difficulty. I pray that if you haven't yet felt the love He has for you, you will begin to feel His compassion and caring for you. Amen

We all have the opportunity.

You may be like me. I like this passage. In fact, it's one of my favorites. There are some passages that are tough to live up to but this one gives us something we all can do. We can all ask for wisdom. We can want to do what God wants us to do. From a tender age, I wanted to be like Solomon. I can remember praying when I was younger over and over for this kind of wisdom. I have prayed often that God would help me, help me to help someone, help me know what to do, help me to accomplish a task. I have prayed often to know what was God's will when it wasn't obvious, and sometimes when it was obvious but I didn't like what he wanted of me.

I read a book once that said that it is a little pompous or arrogant to ask God to help us. Instead, we ought to ask God if we can help Him. I felt embarrassed when I read this book, that my best efforts were so arrogant, even a bit pompous. It had not occurred to me to ask God if I could help Him. I began then to alter my thinking. Solomon's humble prayer is a model prayer for all of us. Solomon was asking for help to do what God had already given him to do. The problem comes in when much of our prayer time is taken up with instructing God on what to do: "Look after my family. Keep my soul as I sleep." These are the kinds of prayers we were taught. But we can also remember Solomon's humble prayer and use it as a guide for our own.

That the Lord spoke to Solomon is not unique. God often speaks to us. Sometimes He speaks to us in dreams, sometimes in a voice we hear: "Go there, help her; be kind; make a commitment; stop." Interestingly, God spoke to Solomon even though Solomon was in the middle of sin. Verse 4 reads," The king went to Gibeon to sacrifice there, for that was the principal high place . . ." Solomon offered a thousand burnt offerings upon this altar, something he had no business doing. He was reflecting the influence of his wife, a non-believer. As I studied this passage, it became clear that God ignored the sin Solomon was into in order to heal him and give him a chance to feel cared about.

Hasn't the Lord spoken to many of us when we were about to do something wrong? You had to decide. Who were you going to follow? Would you listen to God speaking to you or would you ignore His voice? The message may have come in a dream or in a voice saying, "Stop! Go the other direction. Walk away from sin." If it has been a long time since the Lord reached out protectively to you that way, it may be time for repentance so that you can start clean. We all have the opportunity to repent, confess our sins to God, or another person, or both, and to receive communion and know that we are forgiven.

When you ask to be clean through confession, repentance and communion, you are asking God to lead you in the right direction. That is a very good prayer, like Solomon's model prayer. Solomon praised God for how He had blessed his father David and how He helped David to be righteous. Then Solomon did something that Jesus told us years later that we need to do to enter the kingdom of Heaven. Solomon said, " . . . I am only a little child; I do not know how to go out or come in." Solomon was admitting his humility and his child-like faith. You remember what Jesus said in Mark 10:15 (and Luke 18:17), "Truly I tell you, whoever does not receive the kingdom of God as a little child, will never enter it."

Solomon was making himself humble or poor in spirit. He recognized that without God's help he couldn't do anything. That's part of the deep, deep wisdom in the 12 steps. We admit that we are powerless, that we can't and that God can. At the core of all sin is an attitude of "I'll do it myself," an attitude that says, "I don't need God." It says, "I have the ability to do it on my own." It is arrogant; it is an attitude that ignores God and God's Word. If I am the supreme ruler of my life, what do I need with God's direction, guidance or instruction? If I am a child of God, I look to God.

Solomon made a request of God that is the same as ours when we are being sincere and faithful. He asked in verse 9, "Give your servant therefore an understanding mind to govern your people, able to discern between good and evil; for who can govern this your great good people?" The phrase "understanding mind" is understood to refer to wisdom. Yet a literal translation of the Hebrew gives a clearer meaning. The word means literally a hearing heart. Solomon asked for a heart that would obey God. In Solomon's deepest desire was the urge to be completely obedient. Unfortunately, though, he didn't really understand forgiveness. Unlike his father David, he didn't understand that he could go to God for forgiveness and start over. Though his heart was in the right place, Solomon fell out of control because he didn't depend on God's forgiveness to make him clean. He depended on earthly pleasures and on his own intelligence.

We can learn from Solomon's success and his failure. We can approach God like a little child. There is probably not a better way. Jesus said to let the little children come to him. You can be one of these children. If you need forgiveness to be able to really feel accepted, then know that you can have it.

It is my prayer that we will all remember how much God loves us and wants us to succeed. I pray especially that we will reach out to one another and encourage one another in our Christian walk. Amen.

Being A Mature Christian
Ezek 33:7-9, Rom 8-10, Mt 15-20

It's not just a job.

This passage is advanced Christianity—for mature believers. Here, Ezekiel is made a watchman for the house of Israel. As believers—like Ezekiel—we have been made watchers for the church. "Whenever you hear a word from my mouth, you shall give them warning from me." In other words, we are entrusted by God to tell others. Being a believer is not just a job. It is a calling. As believers, we are called to a ministry to reach out to others.

First aid teaches that in the moment of a crisis, thoughts tend to go through our head like, "I don't want to get involved," or "Someone else will take care of it," or "Surely someone who is better qualified will do it." But this passage tells us that there is no calling without responsibility. It is all right for us to do what we can to try to save someone. If you see that it needs to be done, the job is yours. In fact, we're told here that if we don't act, the other person's sins will be attributed to us.

Many of us don't want to do this. The idea of it feels uncomfortable. We don't want to tell people about their sins. Neither did Ezekiel, Jeremiah, Moses, Isaiah, Amos, Ruth or Esther. You remember the story, don't you? Esther had become queen to a Persian king. Some untrustworthy assistants had tricked the king, and Esther's uncle is telling her that she needs to speak up in order to save her people and save the king. Esther is frightened and doesn't want to do it. Her uncle says, "Who knows whether it was not for such a time as this that you were made queen?" (Esther 4: 14)

There are some guidelines for speaking to someone about their sin. It's not about going to their boss or getting them in trouble. We're not telling on them. We can relax about that. We're really only sent to believers to speak about sin. It is not our responsibility to point out mistakes to nonbelievers. Finally, we're to approach a person with humility in our hearts. The idea is to be uplifting to a person. We can help him or her see a negative behavior in a new way.

You may be thinking that you do not feel capable, worthy or knowledgeable enough to do this. Remember, neither did any of the prophets. You may remember Isaiah's words, "Woe is me, for I am lost for I a man of unclean lips and I dwell in the midst of unclean lips." It sounds to me as if he didn't feel he was worthy, either. Isaiah was the only prophet who volunteered. He was not only aware of the sins of those around him, he was aware of his own. When people I have counseled have expressed similar sentiments, I've often told them that it is their self-doubt that qualifies them to carry the message.

Our awareness of our own sin can give us humility. It helps to be humble when approaching a friend, family member or co-worker. Few people like know-it-alls or sanctimonious and self-righteous Sallies telling them to change. Self-righteous Sally is only making herself unwelcome and disliked. I think self-righteous Sally feels guilt and shame like the rest of us but just doesn't want to admit it. She hopes that by telling others she can raise her own self-esteem. Jesus told us to approach others lovingly, not as superior or inferior but as equals.

One of the Seraphim directed by God gave Isaiah permission to fulfill his responsibility. God took Isaiah's guilt seriously. Verse 7 says, "Then one of the seraphim flew to me having in his hand a burning coal which he had taken with tongs from the altar and he touched my mouth and said, 'Behold, this has touched your lips; your guilt is taken away and your sin is forgiven.'" God will do the same for you.

I am reminded of an inmate at the Kentucky Correctional Institute for Women who was a very serious liar. This woman lied, it seemed, about everything. As you can well imagine, she wasn't very popular. Many of us tried to help her. I brought her lying to her attention in every way I knew. Nothing worked. One day she and a volunteer were in the chapel. The volunteer spoke her name and then said, "You seem to have a lying problem. I used to, too. Some friends of mine prayed for me, and God delivered me from lying. Would you like me to pray for you?" The woman was shocked by this and blurted out, "Yes." The three of us prayed together holding hands in a circle. Do you know that that woman never again lied in my presence? She had experienced healing because the sensitive and loving words of the volunteer had reached her.

We also have a responsibility to be willing to listen to other believers who come to us about our mistakes. This is one of the things I most appreciated and respected about Betty Kassulke, the longtime warden at the KCIW and my boss for many years. She was always willing to listen when people told her how she or some part of corrections wasn't doing the right thing. She expected that you would care enough to speak up. This is real leadership—to be willing to hear about our mistakes as well as our achievements. Faithful leaders are willing to listen to the truth.

It is my prayer that each of us will feel God's love so powerfully that we will share that love with people we encounter and that they will see and feel God's love in us. I also pray that we will be faithful in our prayer life so that our sincerity and commitment to God begins to show even more brightly. Amen.

Bibliography

Books

Allen, Roger E., and Allen, Stephen D. *Winnie-the-Pooh on Problem Solving.* New York: Dutton, 1995.

Arndt, William F., and Ginrich, F. Wilbur. *A Greek-English Lexicon of the New Testament and other Early Christian Literature.* Chicago: Zondervan, 1957.

Bandler, Richard, and Grinder, John. *Frogs into Princes: Neuro-Linguistic Programming.* Moab, Utah: Real People Press, 1979.

_____. *Patterns of the Hypnotic Techniques of Milton H. Erickson, M.D.* Cupertino, California: Meta Publications, 1975.

Barber, Joseph, ed. *Hypnosis and Suggestion in the Treatment of Pain: A Clinical Guide.* New York: W.W. Norton, 1996.

Barker, Philip. *Using Metaphors in Psychotherapy.* New York: Brunner/Mazel, 1985.

Benson, Herbert. *Timeless Healing: The Power and Biology of Belief.* New York: Scribner, 1996.

Brown, Francis, Driver, S. R., and Briggs, Charles A. *A Hebrew and English Lexicon of the Old Testament.* Oxford: Claredon Press, 1976.

Buttrick, George Arthur, et al., eds. *The Interpreter's Dictionary of the Bible. Volumes 1,2,3,4 and Supplementary Volume.* Nashville,TN: Abingdon Press, 1962.

_____. *The Interpreter's Bible: A Commentary in 12 Volumes.* Nashville,TN: Abingdon Press, 1952.

Cohen, Abraham. *Everyman's Talmud: The Major Teachings of the Rabbinic Sages.* New York: Schocken Books, 1949 and 1995.

Dolen, Yvonne M. *A Path with a Heart: Ericksonian Utilization with Resistant and Chronic Clients.* New York: Brunner/Mazel, 1985.

Dossey, Larry. Healing Words: The Power of Prayer and the Practice of Medicine. SanFrancisco: Harper, 1993.

Dossey, Larry. *Prayer is Good Medicine: How To Reap The Healing Benefits of Prayer.* San Francisco: Harper, 1997.

Durbin, Paul. *Human Trinity Hypnotherapy.* Michigan: Access Publishing, 1993.

_____. *Kissing Frogs: The Practical Uses of Hypnotherapy.* Dubuque, Iowa: Kendal Hunt Publishing, 1996.

Edgette, John H., and Edgette, Janet Sasson. *The Handbook of Hypnotic Phenomena in Psychotherapy.* New York: Brunner/Mazel, 1995.

Erickson, Milton H., and Rossi, Ernest L. *Experiencing Hypnosis: Therapeutic Approaches to Altered States.* New York: Irvington Publishers, 1981.

_____. *Hypnotherapy: An Exploratory Casebook.* New York: Irvington Publishers, 1979.

Figley, Charles R. *Compassion Fatigue: Coping with Secondary Traumatic Stress Disorder in Those Who Treat the Traumatized.* New York: Brunner/Mazel 1995.

Frankel, Viktor E. *Man's Search For Meaning: An Introduction to Logotherapy.* Boston: Beacon Press, 1959 and 1962.

Fossum, Merle A., and Mason, Marilyn J. *Facing Shame: Families in Recovery.* New York: W.W. Norton, 1989.

Gilligan, Stephen G. *Therapeutic Trances: The Cooperation Principle in Ericksonian Hypnotherapy.* New York: Brunner/Mazel, 1987.

Gordon, David. *Therapeutic Metaphors: Helping Others Through The Looking Glass.* Cupertino, CA: Meta Publications, 1978.

Grinder, John, and Bandler, Richard. *Trance-Formations: Neuro-Linguistic Programming and the Structure of Hypnosis.* Moab, Utah: Real People Press, 1981.

Haley, Jay. *The Power Tactics of Jesus Christ.* Rockville, MD: Triangle Press, 1986.

_____. *Uncommon Therapy: A Casebook of an Innovative Psychiatrist's Work in Short Term Therapy.* New York: W.W. Norton, 1973.

_____, ed. *Advanced Techniques of Hypnosis and Therapy: Selected Papers of Milton H. Erickson M.D.* Orlando, FL: Grune and Stratton Publishers, 1967.

_____, ed. *Conversation with Milton H. Erickson M.D., Volumes I, II, III.* Rockville, MD: Triangle Press, 1985.

Hanlon, Hudson O., and Hexum, Angela L. (comp.). *An Uncommon Casebook: The Complete Clinical Work of Milton H. Erickson.* New York: W.W. Norton, 1990.

Havens, Ronald A., and Walters, Catherine. *Hypnotherapy Scripts: A Neo-Erickson Approach to Persuasive Healing.* New York: Brunner/Mazel 1989.

_____. *The Wisdom of Milton H. Erickson.* New York: Irvington Publishers, 1985.

Heusden, Amy Van, and Eerenbeemt, Elsemarie Van Den. *Balance in Motion: Ivan Boszormenyi-Nagy and His Vision of Individual and Family Therapy.* New York: Brunner/Mazel, 1987.

Hirshberg, Caryle, and Barasch, Marc Ian. Remarkable Recovery: What Extraordinary Healings Tell Us About Getting Well and Staying Well. New York: Riverhead Books, 1995.

Hoorwitz, Aaron Noah. *Hypnotic Methods in Non-Hypnotic Therapies.* New York: Irvington Publishers, 1989.

Keck, Leander E., et al, eds. *The New Interpreter's Bible. Volumes 1,2,3,4,5,7,8,9,12.* Nashville, TN: Abingdon Press, 1994.

Kittel, Rudolf, ed. *Biblia Hebraica.* Stuttgart,Germany: Wurttembergische Bibelanstalt, 1973.

Kolatch, Alfred J. *The Jewish Book of Why.* New York: Jonathan David Publishers, 1981and 1995.

Langs, Robert. *The Therapeutic Interaction; A Synthesis.* New York: Jason Arsonson Inc., 1977.

Lankton, Carol H., and Lankton, Stephen R. *Tales of Enchantment: Goal Oriented Metaphors for Adults and Children in Therapy.* New York: Brunner/Mazel, 1989.

Lankton, Stephen R., ed. *Ericksonian Monographs Number 1: Elements and Dimensions of an Ericksonian Approach.* New York: Brunner/Mazel, 1985.

_____, ed. *Ericksonian Monographs Number 2: Central Themes and Principles of Ericksonian Therapy.* New York: Brunner/Mazel, 1987.

Lankton, Stephen R., and Zeig, Jeffrey K., eds. *Ericksonian Monographs Number 3: Treatment of Special Populations with Ericksonian Approaches.* New York: Brunner/Mazel, 1988.

_____, eds. *Research, Comparisons, and Medical Applications of Ericksonian Techniques.* New York: Brunner/Mazel, 1988.

Lentz, John. *Effective Handling of Manipulative Persons.* Springfield, IL: Charles C. Thomas Publishers, 1989.

Lentz, John. *How The Word Heals.* Lincoln, NE: Writers Press, 2002.

Marlatt G. Alan, and Gordon R. Judith. *Relapse Prevention.* New York: Guilford Press, 1985.

Meeks, Wayne, et al, eds. *The HarperCollins Study Bible (New Revised Standard Version).* San Francisco: HarperCollins Publishers, 1993.

Michael, Robert T., Gagnon, John H., Lsumann, Edward O., and Kolata, Gina. *Sex in America: A Definitive Survey.* Boston: Little Brown and Co., 1994.

Morrison, Clinton. *An Analytical Concordance to the Revised Standard Version of the New Testament.* Philadelphia: Westminster Press, 1979.

Moyers, Bill. *Healing and the Mind.* New York: Doubleday,1993.

Ohanlon, Bill, and Wilk, James. *Shifting Contexts: The Generation of Effective Psychotherapy.* New York: The Gilford Press, 1987.

Paul II, John. *Crossing The Threshold of Hope.* New York: Alfred A. Knopf, 1994.

Prochaska, James, Norcross, John, and Diclemente, Carlo. *Changing for Good.* New York: Avon, 1994.

Poe, Harry L. *The Gospel and Its Meaning: A Theology for Evangelism and Church Growth.* Grand Rapids, MI: Zondervan, 1996.

Rhodes, Arnold B. *The Mighty Acts of God.* Atlanta: John Knox Publishers, 1964.

Rosen, Sidney, ed. *My Voice Will Go With You: The Teaching Tales of Milton H. Erickson.* New York: W.W. Norton, 1982.

Rossi, Ernest L., ed. *The Collected Papers of Milton H. Erickson. Volumes I, II, III, IV.* New York: Irvington Publishers, 1980.

Rossi, Ernest L., and Cheek, David B. *Mind Body Therapy.* New York: WW Norton, 1988.

Steere, David. *Spiritual Presence in Psychotherapy: A Guide for Caregivers.* New York: Brunner/Mazel, 1997.

Sparrow, Scott G. *I Am With You Always: True Stories of Encounters With Jesus.* New York: Bantam Books, 1995.

Telushkin, Rabbi Joseph. *Jewish Wisdom: Ethical, Spiritual, and Historical Lessons from the Great Works and Thinkers.* New York: William Morrow and Company, 1994.

Visotzky, Burton L. *Reading The Book: Making The Bible a Timeless Text.* New York: Schocken Books Inc., 1996.

Wallas, Lee. *Stories for the Third Ear.* New York: W.W. Norton, 1985.

Watzlawick, Paul, Bavelas, Janet Beavin, and Jackson, Don. *Pragmatics of Human Communication: A Study of Interactional Patterns, Pathologies, and Paradox.* New York: WW Norton, 1990.

Watzlawick, Paul. *Munchhausen's Pigtail or Psychotherapy and "Reality."* New York: WW Norton, 1990.

Weil, Andrew. *Spontaneous Healing.* New York: Albert A. Knopf, 1995.

Zeig, Jeffrey K. *Experiencing Erickson: An Introduction to the Man and His Works.* New York: Brunner/Mazel, 1985.

_____, ed. *A Teaching Seminar with Milton H. Erickson.* New York: Brunner/Mazel, 1980.

_____, ed. *Ericksonian Methods: The Essence of the Story.* New York: Brunner/Mazel, 1994.

_____, ed. *Ericksonian Psychotherapy Volume 1.* New York: Brunner/Mazel, 1985.

_____, ed. *The Evolution of Psychotherapy: the Second Conference.* New York: Brunner/ Mazel, 1985.

Zeig, Jeffrey K., and Gilligan, Stephen G., eds. *Brief Therapy Myths, Methods, and Metaphors.* New York: Brunner/Mazel, 1990.

_____, eds. *Developing Ericksonian Therapy State of the Art.* New York: Brunner/Mazel, 1988.

Audio/Video Sources

Andreas. "Eliminating a Compulsion." Presented at the Brief Therapy Conference of the Milton H. Erickson Foundation. San Francisco, CA, 11-15 December 1996. BT96:J241-D13.Videocassette.

Baumann. "Hypnotherapy with Children in a Pediatric Practice." Presented at the Third   International Congress of the Milton H. Erickson Foundation, Phoenix, AZ, 3-7 December 1986. 3rdIC86:PS317-W21AB. Audiotape.

Combs and Freedman. "How Did Erickson Get People To Do Those Things? Utilizing Clients' Response." Presented at the Third International Congress of the Milton H. Erickson Foundation, Phoenix, AZ, 3-7 December 1986. 3rdIC86:PS317-SC5. Audiotape.

Dolan. "The Legacy of the February Man: Ericksonian Age Regression Techniques." Presented at the Third International Congress of the Milton H. Erickson   Foundation, Phoenix, AZ, 3-7 December 1986. 3rdIC86:PS317-W23AB. Audiotape.

Erickson-Elliott, Erickson, Erickson, and Erickson. "How Milton H. Erickson Encouraged His Children to Develop Individuality." Presented at the Third International Congress of the Milton H. Erickson Foundation, Phoenix, AZ, 3-7 December 1986. 3rdIC86:PS317-TP11. Audiotape.

Erickson, Erickson, Lankton, and Rossi. Keynote Panel: "Erickson's Use of Humor." Presented at the Third International Congress of the Milton H. Erickson Foundation, Phoenix, AZ, 3-7 December 1986. 3rdIC86:PS317-K1. Audiotape.

Gilligan. "Love in the Face of Violence: A Self-Relational Approach to
    Psychotherapy." Presented at the Brief Therapy Conference of the
    Milton H. Erickson Foundation, San Francisco, CA, 11-15
    December 1996. BT96:J241-W84AB. Videocassette.

Gilligan, Lange, and Sherman, Stern. "Resistance." Presented at the Third
    International Congress of the Milton H. Erickson Foundation,
    Phoenix, AZ, 3-7 December 1986. 3rdIC86:PS317-TP2. Audiotape.

_____. "Symptom Phenomena as Trance Phenomena." Presented at
    the Third International Congress of the Milton H. Erickson
    Foundation, Phoenix, AZ, 3-7 December 1986. 3rdIC86:PS317-
    W28AB. Audiotape.

_____. "The Courage to Love: A Self-Relations Demonstration."
    Presented at the Brief Therapy Conference of the Milton H.
    Erickson Foundation, San Francisco, CA, 11-15 December 1996.
    BT96:J241-D15.Videocassette.

Gordon. "Therapeutic Metaphor." Presented at the Third International
    Congress of the Milton H. Erickson Foundation, Phoenix, AZ, 3-7
    December 1986. 3rdIC86:PS317-W25AB. Audiotape.

Haley, Rossi, and Zeig. "Conversation Hour: About Milton Erickson."
    Presented at the Evolution of Psychology Conference of the Milton
    H. Erickson Foundation, Las Vegas, NV, 13-15 December 1995.
    EVOL95:MH260-CH7.

Lankton. "Clinical Use of Trance Phenomena for Therapy and Pain
    Control." Erickson Selected Seminars/Congress Tapes of the Milton
    H. Erickson Foundation. One Hour Demo. 1983 Congress:
    V8186-83B. Videocassette.

_____. "Hypnosis in Marriage and Family Therapy." Presented at the
    Third International Congress of the Milton H. Erickson Foundation,
    Phoenix, AZ, 3-7 December 1986. 3rdIC86:PS317-W43AB.
    Audiotape.

_____. "Methods of Constructing Sophisticated Metaphors for Specific
    Outcomes of Affect." Presented at the Third International Congress
    of the Milton H. Erickson   Foundation, Phoenix, AZ, 3-7 December
    1986. 3rdIC86:PS317-W4AB. Audio tape.

O'Hanlon. "Directive Couples Counseling." Presented at the Third
    International Congress of the Milton H. Erickson Foundation,
    Phoenix, AZ, 3-7 December 1986. 3rdIC86:PS317-W7AB. Audiotape.

Polster and Zeig. "Heroism." Presented at the Evolution of Psychology Conference of the Milton H. Erickson Foundation, Las Vegas, NV, 13-15 December 1995. EVOL95:MH260-D11. Audio tape.

Relinger. "Indirect Suggestions in the Treatment of Depression." Presented at the Third International Congress of the Milton H. Erickson Foundation, Phoenix, AZ, 3-7 December 1986. 3rdIC86:PS317-SC29. Audiotape.

Rosen. "Group Induction." Presented at the Third International Congress of the Milton H. Erickson Foundation, Phoenix, AZ, 3-7 December 1986. 3rdIC86:PS317-GI-3. Audiotape.

_____. "Mind Reading." Presented at the Third International Congress of the Milton H. Erickson Foundation, Phoenix, AZ, 3-7 December 1986. 3rdIC86:PS317-W45AB. Audiotape.

Rossi. "Creative Life Facilitation with Hypnotherapy." Presented at the Third International   Congress of the Milton H. Erickson Foundation, Phoenix, AZ, 3-7 December 1986. 3rdIC86:PS317-W3AB. Audiotape.

_____. "Research Frontiers in the Evolution of Psychotherapy." Presented at the Evolution of Psychotherapy Conference of the Milton H. Erickson Foundation, Anaheim, CA, 12-16 December 1990. EVOL90:PC289-W21AB. Audiotape.

Rossman. "Listening To Your Symptom." Presented at the Brief Therapy Conference of the Milton H. Erickson Foundation, San Francisco, CA, 11-15 December 1996. BT96:J241-D2. Videocassette.

Shapiro. "Trance on Trial: The Legal Implications of Ericksonian Hypnotherapy." Presented at the Third International Congress of the Milton H. Erickson Foundation, Phoenix, AZ, 3-7 December 1986. 3rdIC86:PS317-SC14. Audiotape.

Simpson III. "Diagnosing: Reframing to Help Parents Establish a Context for Change." Presented at the Third International Congress of the Milton H. Erickson   Foundation, Phoenix, AZ, 3-7 December 1986. 3rdIC86:PS317-SC33. Audiotape.

Thompson. "Conversational Induction with Utilization of Spontaneous Trance." Erickson Selected Seminars/Congress Tapes of the Milton H. Erickson Foundation. 1983 Congress: V8186-83F. Videocassette.

Watzlawick. "Psychotherapy of 'As If.'" Presented at the Evolution of
    Psychotherapy Conference of the Milton H. Erickson Foundation,
    Anaheim, CA, 12-16 December 1990. EVOL90:PC289-W26AB.
    Audiotape.

Watzlawick and Madanes. "The Construction of Therapeutic Realities."
    Presented at the Evolution of Psychotherapy Conference of the
    Milton H. Erickson Foundation, Anaheim, CA, 12-16 December
    1990. EVOL90:PC289-12. Audiotape.

Weakland and Fisch. "Off the Pedestal: Advantages and Limitations in
    Erickson's Work." Presented at the Third International Congress of
    the Milton H. Erickson Foundation, Phoenix, AZ, 3-7 December
    1986. 3rdIC86:PS317-W50AB. Audio tape.

Wilson. "Strategic Interventions in Panic Disorder." Presented at the Third
    International   Congress of the Milton H. Erickson Foundation, Phoenix,
    AZ, 3-7 December 1986. 3rdIC86:PS317-W26AB. Audiotape.

Yapko. "Building Expectancy." Presented at the Fifth International
    Congress of the Milton H. Erickson Foundation, Phoenix, AZ, 2-6
    December 1992. 5thIC92:ME297-4*s. Videocassette.

_____. "Ericksonian Approaches in the Treatment of Depression."
    Presented at the Third International Congress of the Milton H.
    Erickson Foundation, Phoenix, AZ, 3-7 December 1986.
    3rdIC86:PS317-W11AB. Audiotape.

Zeig. "Brief Ericksonian Psychotherapy." Presented at the Brief Therapy
    Conference of the Milton H. Erickson Foundation, San Francisco,
    CA, 11-15 December 1996. BT96:J241-D1. Videocassette.

_____. "Ericksonian Hypnotherapy." Presented at the Third
    International Congress of   the Milton H. Erickson Foundation,
    Phoenix, AZ, 3-7 December 1986. 3rdIC86:PS317-W30AB.
    Audiotape.

_____. "Fundamentals of Ericksonian Therapy." Presented at the
    Evolution of   Psychotherapy Conference of the Milton H. Erickson
    Foundation, Anaheim, CA, 12-16 December 1990.EVOL90:PC289-
    W33AB. Audiotape.

_____. "Guiding Associations." Presented at the Evolution of
    Psychology Conference of the Milton H. Erickson Foundation, Las
    Vegas, NV, 13-15 December 1995. EVOL95:MH260-CP1.
    Audiotape.

_____. "Symbolic Hypnotherapy." Erickson Selected Seminars/Congress Tapes of the Milton H. Erickson Foundation. 2 hours, 40 minutes. 1978 Symbols:V8184-8A. Videocassette.

_____. "The Personal Growth and Development of the Brief Therapist: Developing . . ." Presented at the Brief Therapy Conference of the Milton H. Erickson Foundation, San Francisco, CA, 11-15 December 1996. BT96:J241-W87AB. Videocassette.

Zeig and Masterson. "Ericksonian Methods: The Virtues of Our Faults." Presented at the Evolution of Psychotherapy conference of the Milton H. Erickson Foundation, Anaheim, CA, 12-16 December 1990. EVOL90:PC289-11. Audiotape.

Epilogue

I hope this book has helped you as you work through whatever difficulties face you in your life. You might pick it up occasionally when you need additional support and to remember its positive messages about you and your life. I encourage you to keep your Bible close at hand and to read it frequently. You might also want to keep other positive reminders around you. These things might include other inspirational books, photographs of loved ones or a letter from a good friend. The people who maintain the positive changes they make recognize that they will always need support. Their humility is what keeps them strong.

Prayer is one of God's greatest gifts to us. Accept it, use it, rely on it, and immerse yourself in it to be close to Him. He has given it to us because He loves us.

Now may the Lord bless you and keep you. May He make His face to shine upon you and give you peace.

Amen.

About the Author

John D. Lentz, D. Min., is both a licensed therapist and an ordained minister. His ministry includes directing the Ericksonian Institute of Jeffersonville, Indiana, where he practices marriage and family therapy, and teaching hypnosis for use in clinical settings. A second part of his ministry is writing and producing outreach materials, including books, tapes and CDs, to assist people in using their faith to overcome life difficulties.

Dr. Lentz retired from the Kentucky Correctional Institute for Women after serving as chief chaplain for 22 years. For 18 of those years, he also served as adjunct professor at the Louisville Presbyterian Theological Seminary, where he taught clinical aspects of counseling, including understanding the dynamics of abusive family systems.

He is a member in good standing with the Mid-Kentucky Presbytery, and has supervisory status in the following organizations: The American Association of Marriage and Family Therapy (AAMFT); the American Society for Clinical Hypnosis (ASCH); and the American Association for Pastoral Counselors (AAPC). He is also a member of the International Society for Clinical Hypnosis and the International Medical and Dental Hypnotherapy Association.

Dr. Lentz has presented at a number of national and international meetings on subjects that include: The Bible and Hypnosis; Spirituality; and Safety From Seduction. Clinical topics have included: Impossible Patients; Systemic Aspects of Abuse; Self-Care of the Therapist; Women Who Murder; and Managing Manipulation.

He is also the author of two previous books, *How the Word Heals*, published by Writers' Club Press, 2002; and *Effective Handling of Manipulative Persons*, published by C. Charles Thomas, Springfield, Illinois, 1986.

Tapes and CDs designed to enhance the listener's faith while providing assistance are available on the following topics:

Freedom From Migraines	Self-Hypnosis for Chronic Pain
Using Anger in Healthy Ways	Freedom from Tobacco
Feeling Forgiven	Help for Psoriasis
Achieving Prosperity	Treating Tinnitus
Freedom From Criticism	Driving to Relax

Dr. Lentz is also available for personal appearances and teaching seminars. He can be reached at Lentzhome@aol.com